PEAKS

THE STORY OF THE
BOB GRAHAM ROUND
AND BEYOND

Peter McDonald

First published in 2021

ISBN 978-1-80068-018-0

Based on *42 Peaks: The Story of the Bob Graham Round* first published in the UK 1982 (written by Roger Smith; revised by Paddy Buckley and Brian Covell). Revised editions published 2005, 2007 and 2012

Copyright © Bob Graham 24-Hour Club

No part of this publication may be reproduced, stored or transmitted in any form without prior written permission from the copyright holder

A CIP catalogue record for this book is available from the British Library

CONTENTS

Author's preface	1
Runner's foreword	3
ORIGINS OF THE ROUND	**7**
PUSHING PAST FORTY TWO	**17**
A CLUB IS FORMED	**27**
FIFTY YEARS ON	**43**
A NOTABLE RETIREMENT	**53**
AGE OF ENDURANCE	**63**
2020 AND BEYOND	**77**
Further reading	83
Record tables	85

Richard Askwith · *1,023*

Ged Hunter · *1,026*

Gary Baum · *926*

Anne Johnson · *652*

Steve Birkinshaw · *1,244*

Lawrie Jones · *1,130*

Ann & Billy Bland · *52*

Kilian Jornet · *2,228*

Graham Breeze

Dave Littler

John Brockbank · *324*

Mark McDermott · *375*

David Butterfield · *1,983*

Cerys McDonald

Julie Carter · *1,292*

Carol Morgan · *1,766*

Steve Chilton

Jasmin Paris · *1,980*

Graham Cleminson

Beth Pascall · *2,395*

Wynn Cliff · *16 (associate)*

Adam Perry · *1,405*

Kim Collison · *1,463*

John Price

Cumbria Archives

Lee Procter · *2,015*

Wendy Dodds · *139*

Mike Quinn · *2,155*

Joe Faulkner · *318*

Rucksack Club

Fell and Rock Climbing Club

Nicky Spinks · *1,257*

Andrew Fullwood

Martin Stone · *108*

Jon Gorrigan

Dan Summers · *2,080*

Paul Gregory

Peter Todhunter

Katherine Harrison

Hélène Whitaker · *448*

Mark Hartell · *668*

Bob Wightman · *1,248*

Charmian Heaton

Morgan Williams · *371*

Rob Howard

Paul Wilson · *2,067*

Martin Hudson · *103*

Selwyn Wright · *170*

AUTHOR'S PREFACE

This book is about the origins of the Bob Graham Round, the development of the Lake District 24-Hour Fell Record, the establishment of the Bob Graham Club and the many remarkable achievements that have come since.

There have been well over two thousand Bob Graham completions, each deeply memorable for all involved. It is clearly impossible to tell the story of them all. Instead, the book tells the story of those stories, seeking to convey the unique essence of the Bob Graham community. Reflecting the Bob Graham Club's constitution, I hope it can play a small part in preserving the spirit, tradition and ethics of the Bob Graham Round – and encouraging all aspiring and existing members to do the same.

The first edition of *42 Peaks* was written by Roger Smith in 1982, with a foreword from Harry Griffin and with significant material provided by Fred Rogerson, founding Chairman of the Club. It was published to coincide with the 50th anniversary of Bob Graham's 1932 round. The text was updated with additional material on two further occasions, first by Paddy Buckley in 2005 and then by Brian Covell in 2012.

This new edition celebrates a further 50th anniversary, that of the establishment of the Bob Graham Club in 1971. While it is a wholly new book, I am indebted to each of Roger, Paddy and Brian for the inspiration provided by their original words. Similarly, a large number of members and friends of the Club have helped produce this book – their names are set out opposite. Just like the round itself, the book could not have been completed without their support. Thank you to all.

Peter McDonald

RUNNER'S FOREWORD

You know the feeling: it is a perfect mountain running day, the scenery looks beautiful and you have all the excitement of a big day out as you climb up Skiddaw. It is that lovely running line off Clough Head and towards the Dodds, all spread out ahead of you. The ground and gradient is perfect for you, the trod is just trod enough. This is perfect, you think.

The weather is just right for you, drizzly rain, beaming sunshine, crunchy snow, somewhere in between, you choose. You feel elated, this is going to be a great run, a fantastic day out for you. You are just slightly out of your comfort zone, having taken on this challenge that you did not know you could do; now you are here trying to do it, something inside your head is still questioning your ability to finish, but you are not listening. All you can feel is the ground beneath you, the lovely effort of pushing it away under your shoes, the slightly out of control sensation that drives a lovely adrenaline push.

The round goes on, drifting over the Langdale Pikes, the climb up Bowfell, the rocks of the Scafells. The lovely views of Wast Water as you float away from Scafell Pike. The glory of all of leg four, the uniqueness of Steeple, the flatness of Pillar (how did that mountain top get so flat?), the crags and scramble of big Gable. The tail end three fells of leg five, complete with the wonderful Robbo(-inson). This day is yours, you already have the lovely sensation of leaving it all out there, giving it everything you have. It has been the perfect combination of achievement versus a step out of your comfort zone, it might be your biggest achievement ever.

Opposite: Carol Morgan and Kim Collison descend Great Gable during Kim's 2020 Lake District 24-Hour Fell Record (Steve Ashworth)

Overleaf: Contenders approach the Market Square in Keswick (Jon Gorrigan)

I imagine this is how my pre-Bob mind pictured me doing a round, floating into Keswick on a cloud of self-achievement. The reality is that the hours of reconnaissance in conditions from brilliant sunshine to hammering rain with minimal visibility build the level of resilience necessary to finish a Bob and be 'Queen for a Day' day (when else do other people deal with your stinky feet and carry all your gear up every hill?). The day itself had highs – many highs – and a few lows. I was lucky enough to have the right people to support and encourage me at the right times. I hope you enjoy this journey of self-learning, support and, very importantly, supporting others as much as I did.

I have had writer's block all week about this foreword. How do you write a foreword for a book about the Bob Graham Round – a really good one, that encompasses the history and folklore of the round, what it means to people, and the huge challenge to complete or compete? And how do you put it together in a book that people will read, that does it justice? I have no idea.

I enjoyed this book. I hope you do too. My sincere thanks to those involved in documenting our history of our round. My insincere thanks to Kim (Co-President of the Bob Graham Club) for nominating me to write this!

Carol Morgan
Co-President of the Bob Graham Club

6 · 42 PEAKS

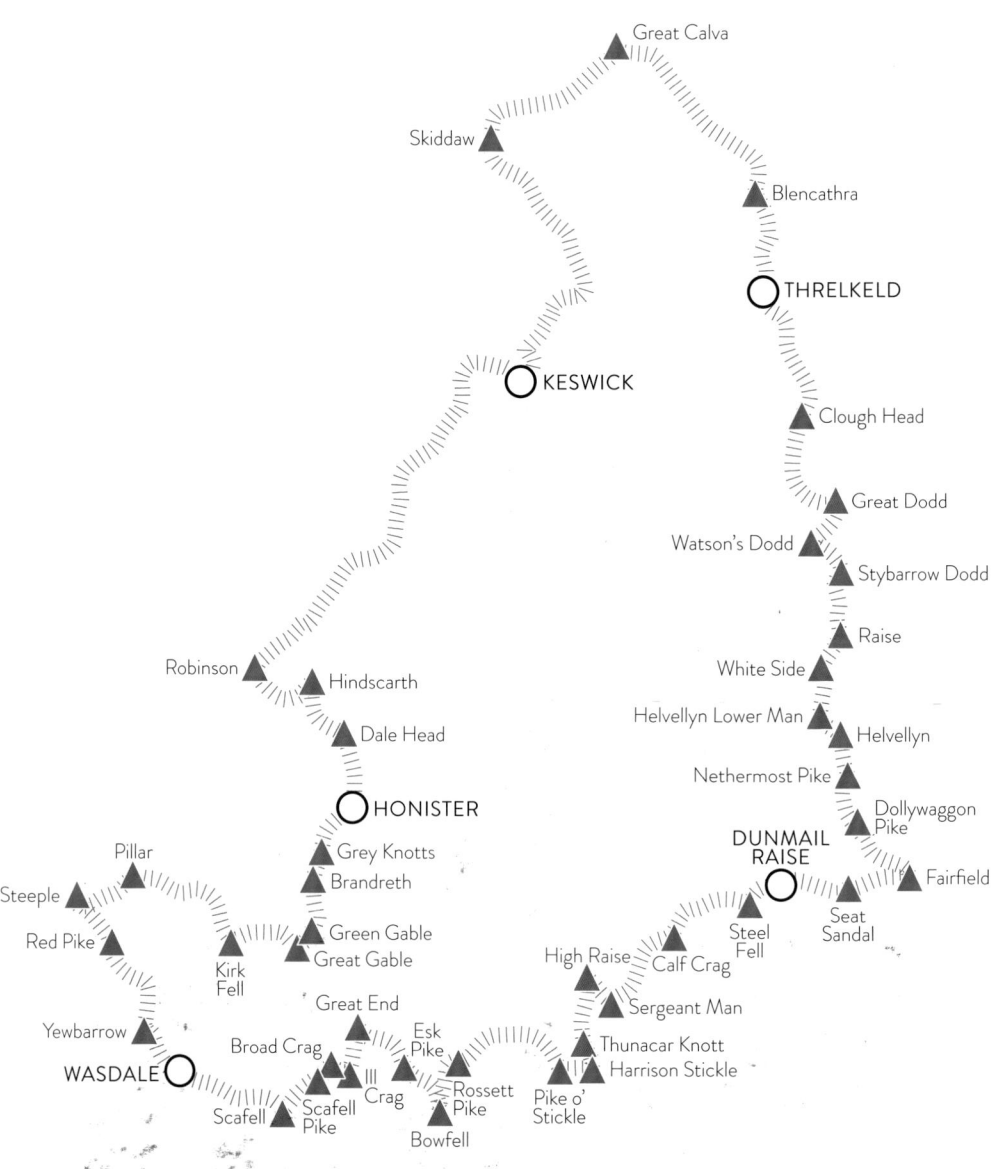

ORIGINS OF THE ROUND

'No doubt it constitutes a stupendous feat in endurance, but it serves little or no purpose. It is not a thing that will be copied, even by the strongest.'

Sheffield Daily Telegraph

On 13 June 1932, Bob Graham set out from the Market Square in Keswick on a warm night under a waxing moon. He was embarking on a challenge which had existed in some fashion for a century. He did not invent the Lake District 24-Hour Fell Record; he was trying to beat it. And so he did: 23 hours and 39 minutes later, he and his pacers completed a round of 42 peaks. Little did he know he had also christened the eponymous Bob Graham Round, which would outlive him and grow in a way that none could imagine.

THE PIONEERS

When 'offcomers' – the local name for visitors to Lakeland – first came to the area, the idea of climbing mountains was largely incomprehensible. The fells were to be surveyed safely from the valleys as distant spectacles of beauty rather than actually climbed. Conquering even one peak was to take one's life in one's hands, especially without the services of a guide.

Happily, by the turn of the nineteenth century, aspirations were rising higher. The Lakeland poets were known for their long excursions over the fells and early tourists such as Captain Joseph Budworth sought to demonstrate that a wide range of fells could be climbed – and survived.

The Reverend Julius Elliott is often cited as the first man to hold the so-called Fell Record. In 1864, he completed an anti-clockwise round of nine fells from Wasdale, akin to an extended Mosedale Horseshoe, with Great Gable, Scafell Pike and Scafell. In terms of peaks gained, the circuit would not be surpassed until the late 1890s. However, it was significantly shorter than several long Lake District walks undertaken in the nineteenth century, which could easily extend to 40 or even 50 miles. There is no clear point at which these began, but a number of early efforts are particularly noteworthy.

The first known of these circular walks was completed in 1832 by Harrison Walker and Joseph Clark, both from Keswick; Scafell, Helvellyn and Skiddaw were gained in 18 hours. Much later, in 1865, three Langdale locals – John Bennett, Fleming Coward and Thomas Grisedale – set out from the Old Dungeon Ghyll Hotel to complete a similar circuit. They visited as many hostelries as they did mountains and on each peak a written 'proof slip' was left, requesting that the finder post it to a local newspaper to verify their achievement. Five years later, Thomas Watson, an accomplished northern sportsman, added Blencathra to the round. Despite the summer season, weather was a major factor: the summit of Scafell Pike was reached in 'a most unwelcome snow-squall' and the ascent of Skiddaw had to be made on hands and knees.

Henry Jenkinson was the first to complete a circuit from which one might start to recognise today's Bob Graham route. Jenkinson was the Wainwright of his day, making his name as the author of a tirelessly researched guidebook on the Lake District. He also campaigned vigorously for access to the fells, proving instrumental to the opening of paths on Latrigg. In 1871, he completed a long walk of what came to be called 'Jenkinson's Six': Great Gable, Scafell Pike, Bowfell, Helvellyn, Blencathra and Skiddaw.

Jenkinson's write-up compares favourably with even the most riveting Bob Graham reports. The attempt went seriously awry after Scafell Pike, when his companion decided to retire, the pair having become lost in mist at Esk Hause for three hours. Thus abandoned, Jenkinson miraculously came across two Langdale shepherds who agreed to guide him to Bowfell summit 'for a liberal pecuniary consideration.' At Wythburn, he understandably stopped for an hour's recovery before taking on the final three summits, only later to be 'overcome by sleepiness at the back of Skiddaw, having to rest for a while at a gamekeeper's cottage.' The local press was at pains to point out that 'the whole of this remarkable journey... was accomplished without the use of wine or spirits.' For all of these reasons, we can perhaps forgive him for completing in just under 25 hours.

One by one, some of Lakeland's finest peaks – including Fairfield, Pillar and Great End – were added to the round over the remainder of the century. As the tally rose, the achievements colloquially became known as the Lake District 24-Hour Fell Record. The record was celebrated in its own right, but it also gives a Cumbrian twist to a much more widespread activity, that of the curiously popular Victorian sport of 'pedestrianism' – essentially competitive long-distance walking.

In parallel, British rock climbers were beginning to appreciate what Lakeland could offer as an alternative to continental Alpinism. The result was a fusion of two worlds; most of the men of pedestrian endeavour were also forging new climbing routes on Cumbrian rock. The names of Edward and Charles Pilkington, Ned Westmorland, Richard Broadrick and Samuel Johnston all feature prominently in the achievements of the time. While they shared a love of Lakeland and endurance, they came from an eclectic range of professions. Whether they were educated gentry, northern industrialists or working men, the Lakes provided neutral and accessible ground, where offcomers and locals could test themselves on the same landscape.

WAKEFIELD'S CODIFICATION

By the turn of the twentieth century, the Fell Record had developed into a serious – and seriously competitive – accolade. This also marked the moment that the challenge was first defined. 'The aim of these walks is to ascend the greatest possible number of peaks above 2,000 feet and to return to the starting point within 24 hours,' wrote Dr Arthur Wakefield in a 1906 article on record walks.

Until Wakefield's pronouncement, it was never entirely clear whether the Fell Record was based on a round of the most peaks, the furthest distance or the greatest ascent – or an unknown combination of the three. From this point forward, peak-bagging was the clear currency. Wakefield had every right to set the terms: he was the then record holder on any metric, breaking it on two occasions in consecutive years. While he was a local physician, he was far from a mountaineering amateur. He went on to participate with George

Mallory in the 1922 Mount Everest expedition, the first British team to set out with the explicit aim of reaching the summit.

Wakefield had developed tremendous physical fitness and stamina over many years. He used a bicycle for professional calls and swam in Derwent Water almost every day of the year. After an initial round of 11 fells in 1904, he pushed himself further in 1905 with an anti-clockwise round of 21 fells in 22 hours and seven minutes, consisting of half the peaks that would later become the Bob Graham Round. While he benefited from perfect August weather, his success came despite a succession of minor calamities: a gammy knee gave way while descending Yewbarrow; he lavishly refreshed himself at a local inn before realising he had no means of payment; he ran short of the verification slips which he was leaving on each summit; and a farmer had to cut open his shoes to relieve pressure on his toes. But he did what mattered and made it round.

A SYSTEM OF MOUNTAIN ENDURANCE

Although over a century ago, there are many modern echoes in Wakefield's round: good progress early on, getting ahead of schedule, pain in the middle part causing concern and delay, the stiff ascent of Scafell, a 'very trying' climb up Fairfield, and eventual triumph, with all the pacers joining the contender for the final run into Keswick. He was also the first to adopt lightweight kit on the fells, wearing a rugby shirt, shorts and plimsolls.

Wakefield's record proved hard to better and many a confident challenger failed. Then, in 1916, one Cecil Dawson went out and beat it – or so he claimed. Dawson was a Manchester man, most famous for his 'bog-trotting' exploits in the Peak District. In the summer of 1916, he succeeded in adding two peaks on the Helvellyn ridge to Wakefield's round. Dawson returned to Keswick in 22 hours and 17 minutes, well within 24 hours although some ten minutes slower than Wakefield.

Top: Dr Arthur Wakefield leading the 1924 dedication of the war memorial at Great Gable summit (by kind permission of the Fell and Rock Climbing Club)

Bottom: Eustace Thomas (second from right; bottom row) and his support team for a 1921 attempt on the Fell Record (by kind permission of the Rucksack Club)

Overleaf: Phil Davidson, Bob Graham and Martin Rylands at Dunmail Raise (George Abraham)

ORIGINS OF THE ROUND • 11

Under the supposed terms of the record, this should not have mattered. However, the community took against him and the prevailing mood was not to endorse it as a record. It is unclear who led the disqualification or for what precise reasons. There was some suggestion that he was not witnessed on each peak, but in all likelihood this was technical cover for a deeper wound: the fact he completed his round during the First World War. Wakefield was preparing for the Somme offensive just as Dawson set out on his walk. By the noble standards of the time, it would have been deemed a highly improper act.

Thankfully, there was no such controversy when Eustace Thomas of the Manchester-based Rucksack Club improved on Wakefield's record in the early 1920s. Thomas's story is one of a remarkable transformation: in his late thirties, he was an unathletic businessman; by the middle of his fifties, he would be one of the most prestigious walkers of the interwar period.

He had not long been introduced to the Lakeland fells, but some inner, ready-kindled fire must have caught aflame, as within a year he was chasing records. In 1920, he succeeded in completing Wakefield's exact round nearly an hour quicker, thus taking the Fell Record. In what has since become a treasured tradition, Thomas was paced by Wakefield, the holder of the very record he was seeking to surpass.

Unsatisfied with his achievement, Thomas made several further attempts to add more peaks, acquiring a large support team who turned crewing into a regular summer holiday. By now, attempts required the professionalism and systematic preparation which is evident in so many of today's endurance challenges. Thomas took this a step further and made it his personal mission to define a 'system of mountain endurance' to train body and mind. He left no stone unturned – from training, to breathing, to nutrition, to sleep, to pacing: his method was the original pursuit of marginal gains.

The 1922 season saw him take the Fell Record to 29 peaks. He was 53 at the time. In addition to Wakefield's 21, he added Great Calva and eight fells along the Helvellyn ridge. After he returned to Moot Hall, Thomas carried straight on after only the briefest of rests, heading up to the Grasmoor massif via Braithwaite to gain five further peaks. While this would not be achieved within the 24 hours, his object was to complete a continuous walk with a total climb in excess of 30,000 feet. This was far more than just a neat number; it was a deliberate act to ascend to a height greater than Mount Everest, intended to show that the Lakeland fells could present just as much of a challenge as any international mountaineering expedition.

This was the context when Bob Graham embarked from Keswick Market Square in an effort to beat Thomas's record. The year was 1931, not 1932. He did not succeed: all that we know is that bad weather and a mistake in route finding caused the attempt to be abandoned.

Graham was determined to try again but, before he could, Freddie Spencer Chapman had introduced himself as the next contender. Chapman was a man whose later career would involve the professions of explorer, mountaineer, soldier, schoolmaster and author. He was led to the Fell Record by Wakefield, who was keen to coach a fellow alumnus of Sedbergh school, and found Chapman to be a willing and hardy protégé. The plan was a circuit of 42 peaks – a huge leap on Thomas's 29 and perhaps based on a route developed by Graham for his abortive attempt.

Setting off in May 1932 and going anti-clockwise, Chapman was met on Bowfell by none other than Bob Graham, hot cocoa in hand and primed to pace him to Dunmail Raise. Sadly, Chapman flagged on the final leg, ultimately becoming enmeshed in bracken while attempting a shortcut down Skiddaw. He made it back to Keswick, but not within the 24 hours. Having come so close, the newspapers promised: 'Mr Chapman hopes to make another attempt on the record in June.' In the end, he did not. But Graham did.

BOB GRAHAM'S ROUND

What kind of man was Bob Graham? He was brought up in Houghton and as a young man worked as a gardener, first in nearby Carlisle and then in Keswick. He had many interests – he conducted choirs, played tennis, studied nature and, of course, loved nothing more than travelling over the fells. While he would not have regarded himself as an athlete, he was a teetotaller, non-smoker and always seemed to move at a fast walk or trot. In the summer, after supper, he would sometimes 'skip up Skiddaw and back', treating it more like a dessert than an exertion.

By the time of the attempt, Graham was running a guesthouse in Keswick and later took over Barrow House in Borrowdale, which is now an independent hostel. The only specific preparation he and his friends undertook before the round was to take long trips over the fells, many of which lasted through the night. The final training walk took them from Keswick to High Street and back again.

Having seen to the needs of his guests, Graham started his round at 1am on Sunday 13 June 1932. The record attempt had been planned for the previous weekend but had been called off because of poor weather. This time nothing was to go wrong. He decided to head clockwise on the advice of George Abraham, mountaineer and pioneering photographer of climbing scenes. As Fred Rogerson later noted, this meant Graham's round was 'all the more remarkable, because all other previous 24-hour rounds, of fewer peaks, had been done anti-clockwise, so he had no yardstick.'

With Martin Rylands – just 18 years old – as pacer, the leg from Keswick to Threlkeld was soon accomplished. The north to south traverse from Clough Head took in two new tops: Nethermost Pike and Seat Sandal. Dunmail was reached at 9.45am and Abraham was waiting with his camera to capture the moment, the product of which is now the centrepiece of the prized Club certificate.

Phil Davidson took over the pacing for the steep pull up Steel Fell, a route Graham inaugurated: until that point, previous records involved a long lowland transition, walking from Fairfield, often via Grasmere, to Langdale and then up The Band to Bowfell. Instead, Bob chose to traverse over the tops, adding eight further peaks, involving an additional 1,000 feet of ascent over fell terrain, albeit little additional distance.

Robin Deans accompanied Graham over the tough Wasdale to Honister stretch, arriving at the quarry at 9.45pm. Now paced by Bill Hewitson, they had just over three hours to climb Dale Head, Hindscarth and Robinson, and get back to Keswick. They descended by High Snab Bank, Robinson's north-western shoulder, before dropping down into Little Town.

The full pacing team came together for the final road run, the four trusty friends jogging through the night streets of Keswick and up to the Moot Hall. It was 39 minutes past midnight; the stocky figure in shirt, shorts and plimsolls had done it. But there was no fanfare, just handshakes among the team. They retired to Graham's guesthouse and at 6am he was up as usual to cook them breakfast.

'I felt fine when we got in,' Bob later recalled. 'The uphill bits gave me a rest, and if I felt tired going up I thought to myself: I can always get a rest coming down the next bit.' He fondly remembered how pleased he felt on the last stretch in the moonlight, realising he was going to crack the record. 'We were laughing and telling tales all the way. We thought it was great fun. Yes, it was a good day.' Years later, when asked what had kept him going, he grinned and said: 'willpower'.

PUSHING PAST FORTY TWO

1933 – 1966

*'Anybody should be able to do it,
providing they are fit enough.'*

Bob Graham

Bob Graham's Fell Record would stand for 28 years. The difficulty of beating it meant there was even a danger of it being forgotten. But once revived, it was never lost again, nurtured by the burgeoning long-distance fell running community in Lakeland, most notably the names of Rogerson, Bradshaw, Heaton and Naylor. Their efforts would see the 42 peaks matched – and surpassed.

THE LONG GAP

In 1933, Bob set out once more. This time, he was trying to better his own record, just like many others before and since. His aim was to reach the landmark 30,000 feet of ascent by adding two or three fells from the Grasmoor range. Frustratingly, he was beaten by hard rain and thick mist on two occasions. His second thwarted attempt ended on Pike o' Stickle, 22 fells and 12 hours into the round. 'I enjoyed what I did do – and I feel fine,' he reflected.

Still, Bob's unfulfilled desire did nothing to detract from the scale of his 1932 achievement. While he sought no publicity, it was celebrated in the local press

Opposite: Bob Graham's gravestone at St Andrew's churchyard in Stonethwaite

and he became well known in Cumbria. Technically, two of the peaks on his round fell foul of Wakefield's 2,000-feet criterion (Steel Fell and Calf Crag) and others were hardly prominent summits (such as High Snab Bank and Thunacar Knott). But the fact that he broke the record so markedly meant there was little grumbling. Inevitably, some doubted whether he had actually done it, perhaps because of the exaggerated distance referenced in many newspapers – some reports claimed the round covered 130 miles (double the true total). This spurious statistic is even inscribed on Bob Graham's gravestone.

Perhaps this figure also dissuaded any would-be contenders as there was seemingly little interest in picking up the gauntlet. Aside from Bob himself, the only exception was a young Colin Dodgson, who made a bid for the record later in 1932 but was forced to abandon at Great End due to injury. The year before, he had completed a round similar to Eustace Thomas's, albeit in a longer time.

Later in life, Bob expressed surprise that no one had beaten his record; he believed that anyone fit and prepared could do as he had. But while described in the local press as a 'long walk', his round had been no perambulation – Bob was probably the first Fell Record holder to run more than he walked. He did so at a time when endurance fell running was largely unknown. While there was a limited calendar of short races, such as at the famous Grasmere Sports, there were no organised long Lakeland events (the first to be established, the Lake District Mountain Trial, would not begin for another twenty years). All told, the combination of the Second World War, the scale of Graham's achievement and steadily waning memories meant the Fell Record lay untouched.

The interlude was only twice interrupted. In 1954, Ted Dance set out to match Bob's 42 peaks in a quicker time, with Bob there to see him off. Ted made good progress over the first fells, but mist and rain necessitated close compass work, which continually slowed his pace. He fell far behind schedule and retired at Langdale. Des Oliver also tried for the record in the summer of 1956. With tongue in cheek, Bob asked the support team to pass on a message partway through the round that Des should try to go beyond 42 peaks in order 'to do the thing properly'. In the end, the banter never landed as bad weather forced him to abandon at Wasdale.

ENTER THE HEATONS

Throughout this period, Harry Griffin played an important role in keeping the memory of Lakeland challenges alive. Harry was one of the most popular writers on the Lake District and a fine mountaineer himself. He liked to remind people of Bob's record in his regular column in the Lancashire Evening Post. One such article was the catalyst for a pivotal event: the entrance of the Heaton brothers.

The 1960 piece was written at a time when Dr Barbara Moore was generating much publicity by walking from Land's End to John o' Groats on a minimalist and vegan diet. Harry felt that 'the long-established Bob Graham record was a far worthier challenge than the road plod, especially for mountain folk.' The article caught the imagination of Alan and Ken Heaton, both members of Clayton-le-Moors Harriers in Lancashire. Both were competent mountaineers, and both knew and loved the Lakeland fells. This was something they could have a go at.

They were not alone in this thought. Maurice Collett and Paul Stewart, both of Kendal Athletic Club, planned an attempt on the record for 13 May 1960. The Moot Hall had yet to assume its totemic status and they chose instead to start from Langdale. It was a very gallant try; they experienced rough weather but battled on to complete the round in 27 hours and 20 minutes.

Meanwhile, the Heatons were planning their attempt. They decided on an anti-clockwise circuit on a 23½-hour schedule, starting soon after the summer solstice to maximise daylight. They were joined by Stan Bradshaw, some fifteen years their elder but no less handy.

Accompanied by pacer Alistair Patten, the contenders departed on a warm morning at 10am in June. In a desire to emulate Bob's round, they started from the Moot Hall, although they reverted to the tradition of going anti-clockwise. Thinking that Bob had descended Robinson to Newlands Hause and not Little Town (he had not), they ran for at least a mile further than necessary before turning to head up the first fell. The error was compounded when Ken removed his glasses to refresh himself at Moss Force, placed them down and they were inadvertently crushed by a stray step. But all pressed on and reached Honister 18 minutes ahead of schedule. They were met there by Bob Graham, now a fit-looking 71-year-old, delighted that someone was at last going seriously for

the record. He claimed that the scorching hot weather was ideal – a view not exactly shared by the runners – and wished them the best of luck.

Over the next leg, the three men were forced to split up. Stan was plagued by cramp and could not keep up with the others; Ken dropped out at Black Sail Pass, in large part because of his inevitably poor vision. Alan continued alone, traversing some of Lakeland's toughest summits at a run with neither water nor food. He reached Wasdale in a bad way, consumed by the heat.

It initially seemed impossible that he might continue. But he was fit and determined: after a 45-minute recovery, he felt sufficiently replenished to go on. At 5pm, still 30 minutes ahead of schedule, he trotted across the fields towards Lingmell Gill for the ascent of Scafell, the longest single climb on the whole round. He would have to cover the 15 summits from Wasdale to Dunmail entirely alone, this being before any requirement to be accompanied on every fell.

He went well, climbing down Broad Stand without aid and dropping into Dunmail just before 11pm, still up on schedule. His shoes were falling apart and had to be changed, but he himself was in strong spirits and hardly sat down as he was refreshed with sweet tea. Miraculously, Ken's glasses had been fixed and so he was able to pace his brother over the Helvellyn range. Meanwhile, Stan had continued but had dislocated his thumb on the descent of Yewbarrow. He somehow managed to get to Dunmail without a torch, but then gracefully retired so the support team could focus their efforts on the Heatons.

Alan had ten hours left to reach Keswick and claim the record. It was a fine night and there was every chance he would come through. The prospects looked even better when he arrived in Threlkeld with six hours left to complete the final three peaks. At 7.30am, he topped Skiddaw. Looking down on Keswick, he knew the record was his. He jogged into the Market Square, clocking in at 22 hours and 18 minutes.

The 1932 record had been broken at last, by well over an hour. It was a supreme achievement, particularly on such a hot day and unaccompanied through the toughest part of the round. 'About time, too,' was Bob Graham's reaction to Alan's success. 'I'm not the least upset the record's gone. It's lasted

Left and right: Ken Heaton and Alan Heaton, respectively
Bottom: Ken Heaton, Alan Heaton and Stan Bradshaw with the Fell Record trophy

much too long. This young fellow has put up a wonderful performance.' It was the end of one era and the start of another. Few then could have envisaged how many would follow the 42-peak circuit over the next 60 years.

By way of epilogue, Stan managed a successful completion only a fortnight later. He set out with Maurice and Paul, who were also seeking to redress their earlier attempt. The Kendal pair were forced to abandon, but Stan carried on. This time there was to be no disappointment: he made it round with over half an hour to spare. It was a tremendous feat at the age of 48, especially so soon after the effort of his previous attempt. It would be the last completion of a 42-peak round for over a decade.

EXTENDING THE FELL RECORD

It is a curiosity of history that the peaks tackled by Bob Graham in 1932 were slightly different from those gained by Alan Heaton in 1960 – and that it was Alan's route which would go on to form the recognised Bob Graham Round. No record exists for how or why this happened, but two possible reasons are that the one-inch Ordnance Survey map from Graham's time did not allow for precise peak marking and that the fell running community's attitude to the route was more art than science. No contemporaneous accounts list Ill Crag, Broad Crag or Grey Knotts as Bob Graham fells, despite the fact he would have passed very close to their summits. These three fells have quietly replaced Hanging Knotts (a subsidiary summit of Bowfell), Looking Stead (sitting between Pillar and Black Sail Pass) and High Snab Bank (Robinson's long north-western ridge), each of which were originally recorded as part of Bob's round. Today, contenders pass within spitting distance of all of them, so it all comes out in the wash.

But while Alan had unknowingly inaugurated the round that is today imprinted on every contender's mind, he joined no club and received no certificate. He had broken the Lake District 24-Hour Fell Record, not the Bob Graham record. His achievement did not spark further completions of the 42 peaks. Instead, what began was a period of intense competition for the overall Fell Record.

Almost exactly a year after his brother's success, Ken stepped forward. The objective was to add a number of fells to Alan's round and he prepared a route of 51 peaks. Sadly, Alan could not run in support as he had torn a tendon while training for the attempt. But a man called Fred Rogerson was on hand to assist. A builder from Windermere, Fred would go on to become one of the keystone figures in the Bob Graham story.

Most of the extra peaks were clustered around Langdale, so the start was set for the Old Dungeon Ghyll Hotel. The conditions could not have been more different from the previous year; much of the round was in mist and there were strong, cold winds throughout. The Scafell massif was particularly dicey and Ken cut his hand on loose scree while descending Deep Ghyll en route to Lingmell, one of his new peaks. Despite this, he was always up on schedule and returned to Langdale at a trot. He finished in 22 hours and 13 minutes, beating Alan's time despite climbing an additional 3,000 feet. The total rest time was over two hours – glacial by modern standards but far from unusual in those days.

Only a year before, beating Bob Graham's record had felt momentous; now, in 1961, nine new peaks had been added to the tally and the talk was of what would come next. But Ken was happy to play only a supporting role from then on. Reflecting on the achievement, he said, 'I have accomplished what I set out to do and do not intend to make any further attempts on the Lake District 24-Hour Fell Record. I will give assistance to anyone making an attempt. Undoubtedly my brother, Alan, will have a go and, in all probability, improve on my record.'

And so it proved. Alan was full of praise for his brother, but he made clear he intended to have another crack. In August 1962, he raised the record to 54 peaks, with just 12 minutes to spare. He had to contend with high winds, rain and some very slippery ground, falling several times and even toppling headfirst into a bog. Alan included all 51 tops from his brother's round, plus Aikin Knott (better known as Ard Crags), Scar Crag and Causey Pike.

He had hoped to find time for Grasmoor and Whiteless Pike, but there was simply no opportunity. It must have been a tough day, for even Alan felt the strain. He later admitted, 'I wouldn't have finished if it hadn't been for the others... It was much worse than two years ago and I wouldn't like to do it again.'

REMEMBERING BEARDIE

Eric Beard was a man willing to have a go at anything, bringing his warmth and mirth everywhere he ran. An outdoorsman through and through, he jobbed his

way around the country to pay for the next adventure, often raising considerable amounts for charity in the process. 'Beardie' was everyone's friend and had little difficulty recruiting help for his record attempt: the Heaton brothers, Stan Bradshaw, Des Oliver and Joss Naylor all joined the team.

In July 1963, Beardie set out from Keswick at 6pm. Progress was seamless – and quick. Having already added Great Rigg earlier in the round, he arrived at Newlands Hause with only the final leg to go, clearly on course to break the record. After Aikin Knott, he dropped into the valley and ascended to the saddle below Sail. He was then due to bear east for Scar Crags and Causey Pike to end the round, just as Alan had done. But the pacing team knew he could do more, as did Eric himself. He was thus persuaded to turn west in order to gain Sail, Crag Hill and Grisedale Pike. This was a good call: Eric returned to Keswick on a fine afternoon with 25 minutes in hand. The record now stood at 56 summits.

Beardie would go on to tackle a string of ever more difficult long-distance challenges, including setting records for the Welsh 3,000s, the Cairngorm 4,000s and the complete traverse of the Cuillin Ridge in Skye. In 1969, this culminated in a continuous run up and between Ben Nevis, Scafell Pike and Snowdon, which he completed in a little over ten and a half days. Tragically, he was killed in a road accident later that year at the age of only 38. It was a huge loss for the ascendant sport. He is still remembered with great affection to this day.

SEVEN TIMES IS ENOUGH

With the record having been taken from the Heatons, it was only natural for Alan to seek to reclaim it. He tried, then tried again and then tried once more – 1964 saw three abortive attempts, each marred by atrocious weather. He was only prepared to make one more bid.

This came in July 1965, when he set off from the Old Dungeon Ghyll Hotel. He was assisted by no fewer than 11 pacers at different times, and all the

Top: Eric Beard, Des Oliver, Stan Bradshaw, Alan Heaton and Ken Heaton on Eric's 1963 Fell Record (Fred Rogerson)

Bottom: Fred Rogerson and Joss Naylor waiting to support Alan Heaton at Wasdale on his 1965 Fell Record (Tommy Orr)

support arrangements were left in the infinitely capable hands of Fred and Margaret Rogerson, by now a traditional roadside fixture.

Alan set off in good weather, but it quickly deteriorated and the sketchy terrain led him to take two falls on the descent to Wasdale. Thereafter, the poor conditions did not relent. There was every chance that this final bid would also end in failure, but the party's fellcraft took them through to Honister. Between Newlands and Keswick, Alan gained nine tops compared to Beardie's four. However, after completing these in good time, he 'bonked' on the relatively short road run from Braithwaite to Keswick, nearly collapsing from a lack of energy.

To the waiting support team, this felt uncannily similar to his arrival in Wasdale back in 1960. But, yet again, he managed to recover, pushing on to the Skiddaw and then Helvellyn ranges. While the dogleg to Fairfield and Great Rigg had to be omitted, he continued back to the Langdales, descending Loft Crag to claim a new record of 60 peaks in 23 hours and 34 minutes. After completing, he remarked: 'I'm sure the record could still be improved given better conditions, but I'll not be trying again, seven times is enough.'

AMONGST THE FELLS HE LOVED

The Lake District 24-Hour Fell Record was now at a level which would have seemed quite impossible only five short years earlier, having been advanced on four occasions by three men of exceptional calibre. These fell runners had all set records, but none other than Alan Heaton had completed 'just' the Bob Graham Round.

The achievements were celebrated in a Fell Record trophy inscribed with the names of all known record holders, beginning in the nineteenth century and with ample space set aside for future accomplishments. It is now on display at the Brockhole Visitor Centre in Windermere.

The trophy was first presented in 1966, the same year that Bob Graham passed away at the age of 76. He was buried in Stonethwaite, at the heart of Borrowdale, his epitaph marking how he lay 'amongst the fells he loved'. Happily, he had lived to witness one of the most exciting periods for 24-hour rounds. But his ultimate legacy had only just begun to flourish.

A CLUB IS FORMED

1967 – 1979

'Some motivation was needed to keep the achievements of [Graham and his supporters] alive, otherwise it might well have been another 28 years before any new attempts were made.'

Fred Rogerson

After a run of annual attempts on the Fell Record, there was now a lull in activity. Fortunately, the hiatus was broken by the establishment of the Bob Graham Club, which encouraged others to take on the 42 peaks. With every completion, Bob's round laid down stronger roots. By the end of the 1970s, it was firmly established as the foremost endurance fell running challenge.

THE BOB GRAHAM 24-HOUR CLUB

Over the course of the 1960s, the revival of Bob Graham's round and the extensions to it created a small but close-knit community of record breakers, pacers and supporters. The fact that Fred and Margaret Rogerson were among its most central figures, despite neither ever running on the fells, is testament to their character and dedication.

The Rogersons had supported nearly every Fell Record attempt of the 1960s. But Fred was starting to wonder for how long the progression could realistically continue. After all, the Fell Record would surely soon be pushed to heights that only a tiny handful could attain. In Fred's own words: 'The [Fell

Record] was now beyond all but a very few, dedicated marathon fell runners.' No attempts had been made since Alan Heaton's 1965 record – would this turn into another 'long gap'?

Around 1970, an idea formed in Fred's mind: a club should be established. The British have a penchant for banding together and, in retrospect, it comes as no surprise that those attempting the ultimate test of the fells would wholly welcome the suggestion. At a Fell Record reunion dinner on 22 January 1971, he sought and secured the approval of all in attendance. Such was the enthusiasm, a committee was immediately assembled with Fred as Chairman, a position he would hold for the next 28 years.

Significantly, the purpose of the Club was not to push the Fell Record ever farther. Instead, the object was to support fell runners seeking to replicate Bob Graham's round of 42 fells. The Club's nurturing of the round was a way to help maintain, promote and celebrate 24-hour challenges, even if the actual Fell Record could not be advanced by mainstream contenders.

But why Bob Graham's round and not that of Alan Heaton, Eric Beard or any other? Bob's record had achieved an enduring prominence because of how long it had taken to be beaten and the community that had been formed in the act of surpassing it. Moreover, 42 peaks in 24 hours seemed to offer the perfect balance between difficulty and feasibility: it was hard – very hard – but it was just about doable. There could be no definitive or scientific proof of this, but fell runners instinctively knew it to be true.

EARLY COMPLETIONS

Thus, the Bob Graham Club and the Bob Graham Round were born – both products of Fred Rogerson's vision and tireless commitment to nurturing what he liked to call 'the fell runners' ultimate'. Not long after, later in 1971, the first attempt on the 42 peaks was made since 1960. The contenders were Mike Walford and Alan Evans, both from Kendal. Like many making their first effort, it was unsuccessful in its own narrow terms, but it proved the beginning of something very important.

The next attempt came only a month later, led by Don Talbot and Peter Walkington, both experienced fell runners who had assisted on previous Fell Records. They started together, but Peter pushed ahead during the latter part of the round and finished in 20 hours and 43 minutes, the then fastest time for the 42 peaks. Don Talbot followed him back to the Moot Hall not long after.

Four weeks later, there was another success, with Michael Meath becoming the youngest person so far to complete the round at the age of 24. Alan Evans started with Michael on his own second attempt, but he succumbed to the bad weather. In contrast, Michael pushed through and was rewarded with a warm, sunlit morning after a clear night over Helvellyn and the Dodds. He traversed the final section in fine style, accompanied by Alan Heaton and Pete Bland.

NAYLOR VERSUS NATURE

Meanwhile, the baton of the Fell Record had been grasped by a tall and long-limbed sheep farmer from Wasdale. This was, of course, Joss Naylor. His introduction to rounds had come when he paced Eric Beard in 1963, but Joss largely chose to concentrate on racing for the initial part of his career. By his mid-thirties, he was ready to contend for longer challenges.

His first attempt in 1970 did not even make it onto the fells. Joss and Alan Heaton had planned for a joint attempt to take the Fell Record to 62 peaks, two more than Alan's 60 fells in 1965. Unfortunately, the weather on the day meant the attempt never began. The false start was remedied the very next year. This time Joss was the sole contender, with Alan in support. He chose to start in Wasdale, only a short way from the family farm at Bowderdale. Conditions were decidedly unpromising: low cloud, rain and a high wind on the tops. Again, the start was postponed, but this time by only an hour.

It was characteristic of Joss's style and abilities that his very first climb was Yewbarrow, the painfully steep and desolate ascent which has claimed many a Bob Graham contender. Honister was reached in just over three hours – a fast time and nearly half an hour up on schedule, despite the poor weather and addition of Base Brown between Green Gable and Brandreth. The legs over the Grasmoor and Skiddaw massifs went even better.

This was just as well, as time was lost in the dark over the Dodds and on wet rocks over the final leg. Alan Heaton joined the pacers from Esk Hause in support of the now tiring contender. After a roped ascent of Broad Stand to gain Scafell, Joss ran straight down to Wasdale, ignoring Lingmell given the time on the clock. Still, 61 peaks was a record and he completed the round with 23 minutes to spare. 'I've been planning to do this for four years and I wanted

to do it when I was 35,' Joss said. 'I never felt weak, never had one touch of cramp, but my legs were stiffening at the end.'

On midsummer weekend one year later, the same man and a similar group were back in Wasdale for another attempt. When the day came, it was one of the foulest weekends in local memory. But there was to be no compromise with the elements: Joss strode up Yewbarrow at the pre-appointed hour. Despite high winds and driving rain, he reached the top in only 25 minutes, setting the tone for the remainder of the round – the man had every intention of overcoming the weather.

Still, it was to be a hard fight. Thick cloud meant the moon was of no assistance in the dark over the Helvellyn ridge. There was no time for Fairfield. On the next leg, Sergeant Man was lost in a murky sea of ill-defined tussocks and mounds. At 2am, in the pitch black, attacked by driving rain and searching through thick mist, the pacing team decided that they had reached the true top. But Joss refused to accept the location and simply ran off to find it himself.

A similar episode was encountered over Pike o' Blisco – 'there was no time for a map, just the instinct of a man who had spent all his life working on these fells,' remembered Chris Brasher, one of the pacing team, as he tried to keep up with Joss. 'The rain drummed on my hood so fiercely as to obliterate thought,' Chris recounted. They went on to lose time on the final leg over the Scafells when the rope was not in place at Broad Stand. The rock was simply too slippery to solo, so they had to go the long way round by Lord's Rake. Nevertheless, there was still time to re-introduce Lingmell to the record (Whiteless Pike was the other new top).

The peaks count had been raised to 63, a superhuman performance. The whole team went back to the Naylor farm to celebrate; even as they said their goodbyes, the incessant rain was still thrashing down. Only a man as impervious and fell-hardy as 'Iron Joss' could have got anywhere near the record in such conditions. Chris later affirmed that Joss's run was 'equal to any of the greatest Olympic races that I have ever seen.'

Top: Alan Heaton and Joss Naylor leaving Honister on Joss's 1971 Fell Record (Tommy Orr)
Middle: Alan, Peter Walkington and Joss return to Wasdale on the 1971 Fell Record (Tommy Orr)
Bottom: Peter, Chris Brasher and Alan Walker waiting for Joss on his 1975 Fell Record

TWO SWANSONGS

Alan Heaton had always thought his 1965 record could be improved. The belief that a man could go further was perhaps what drove him to team up with Joss for the aborted 1970 attempt, despite his repeated and avowed intention to retire from attempts at the record. Perhaps it was also because he was 42 that year, a similar age to Bob Graham on the original round. Ken Heaton had been perfectly content with his single record, but Alan was a different animal. He could not turn his back on the challenge.

Joss's heroics did nothing to dim Alan's desire and he stepped up once more in 1973. He set off from Wasdale in very hot conditions, paced, of course, by Joss. By nightfall, the weather had deteriorated, bringing thick mist and torrential rain. Following a bad navigational error on the Langdales, he was forced to abandon after 49 summits in 19 hours.

1974 brought his next attempt, an anti-clockwise round beginning from Keswick. He made good progress over the early legs, but the schedule was tight throughout. Fairfield was a tough addition – a significant ascent during the night at a late part in the round – but it had been omitted since 1962 and Alan felt strongly that all the Bob Graham peaks should be part of the Fell Record.

Threlkeld was reached at 6.30am on a bright Sunday morning. He had only three hours and a handful of minutes left to cover nearly 15 miles and top his last four summits – a mammoth task. In Keswick, anxious friends and supporters waited at Lairthwaite Road, scanning the summit of Skiddaw and the ridge to Lonscale Fell as the minutes ticked away. But it was not to be. As the clock on Crosthwaite Church chimed 10am, Alan and his pacers came into view on Skiddaw Little Man. Agonisingly, he could have beaten Joss's time – and thus taken the record – if he had dropped Fairfield.

Still, he showed no outward sign of disappointment and put on a sprint finish. A class act to the very end – and this time it really was the end. All told, he was the lead contender on ten attempts over 14 years. His brother Ken summed up their feelings: 'We will for a lifetime remember with pride and satisfaction

Top: Joss Naylor setting off from Keswick in 1975, supported by Alan Walker and Eric Roberts
Bottom: Extracts from Joss's verification cards from his 1975 Fell Record

A CLUB IS FORMED • 33

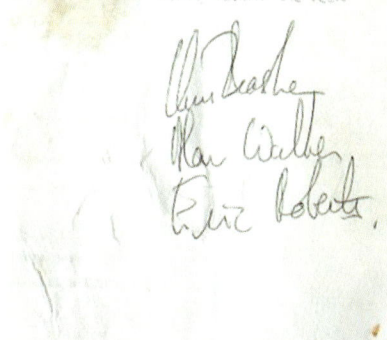

```
CARD ONE                          MIKE AND KEN
  THIRD SECTION. JOS'S BUM BAG/ACC./SWEETS.
                            ARR.        DEP.
   DUNMAIL RAISE.            XXXXXX
 4 Steel Fell_____        13.55       13.55
 5 Calf Crag_____         14.20       14.20
 6 Seargant Man____         14.48       14.48
 7 High Raise_____         14.43       14.43
 8 Thunacar Knott__         14.56       14.56
 9 Pavey Ark_____         15.00       15.00
 0 Harrison Stickle         15.07       15.07
 I Loft Crag_____         15.14       15.14
 2 Pike of Stickle_         15.19       15.19

 3 Rossett Pike____         15.48       15.55 RVa
 4 Pike O Blisco  X         17.23       17.23
 5 Cold Pike_____           ✓           ✓
 6 Red Howe(L.Stand)          ✓           ✓
 7 Crinkle Crag____         17.54
 8 Shelter Crag____         18.09
 9 Bowfell_____         18.15       18.15
 0 Esk Pike_____         18.37
                                          RVb
 Va is D.Talbot at Rossett summit with tea etc.
 Vb is P.Talkington at Esk Hause wall shltr, with
                  Beans,Acc. cake.
      THIS SECTION CONTINUED ON OTHER CARD
```

```
FIFTH SECTION. JOS'S FLY BAG. ALLEN AND CHRIS.
                          ARR.         DEP.
  HONISTER HAUSE  01.00    XXXXXX
 9 Dale Head_____       1.33
 0 Hindscarth_____       1.49
 I Robinson_____       2.10
      NEWLANDS HAUSE     2.25         XXXXXX

 on hand this card to Nobody or Ken.
                      Chris Brian or Ken
                      Chris Brasher
                      Alan Walker
                      Eric Roberts
```

each of the long days on the mountains and in the dales of Lakeland, with friends and companions worthy of the occasion.'

The second swansong came from Joss Naylor, who wanted to set a mark unblighted by conditions. With that in mind, he reached for 72 peaks, no slight increment on his previous record, including five new fells in the Back o' Skiddaw. In stark contrast to 1972, the backdrop was a blistering day, but Joss thrived in the heat.

Starting from Keswick on this occasion, he arrived in Threlkeld after three hours, nine summits topped. Joss's pacers were already struggling to keep up with him – it would prove a regular feature of the day. 'He just isn't human,' remarked one to Fred Rogerson. After the Langdales, Joss broke with tradition and chose not to cross the valley directly to Pike o' Blisco. Instead, he stayed on high ground, inserting Rossett Pike and returning to the usual route via a dogleg from Bowfell. With the inclusion of Fairfield, this meant the Fell Record now incorporated all the Bob Graham peaks.

When he finished, Joss had claimed 72 peaks and with a generous 49 minutes to spare. While both his previous records were a reflection on what could be achieved in spite of conditions, this was a truer measure of his abilities. Even in the context of Joss's legendary achievements, it must be considered one of his most impressive records, alongside that of the Lakes, Meres and Waters, and the Wainwrights Round.

THE MOST EXCLUSIVE CLUB

Membership of the Bob Graham Club can only be gained by completing the round within 24 hours (or a more arduous route, based on the 42 peaks). Chris Brasher once described it as 'the most exclusive club in the world, because you cannot buy your way into it.' The rules are wonderfully simple: all that matters is visiting the peaks within the prescribed period, subject to two conditions. First, contenders must start and finish in Keswick at the Moot Hall. Second, the endeavour must be undertaken in the company of others. This tradition is more than a concern for safety or veracity (important as they are); it reflects the ethos of the Club, which is that the spirit of the round is best preserved by giving and receiving support.

In 1972, two new members joined. The next year, it was five. Then 13, then 14 more. The Bob Graham Round was taking its place as the pinnacle of endurance fell running, at a time when many new long-distance fell races were coming onto the calendar. By the end of 1975, 42 men had joined the Club, four through breaking the Fell Record and 38 by completing the Bob Graham. The proportions clearly justified the decision to separate the overall peaks record from the 42-peak round; it would have been a much smaller club had it been otherwise. Nonetheless, the fact that only around half of all attempts were successful demonstrated that Bob Graham's was the right round to immortalise.

As membership grew, the fastest times fell. In August 1973, Bill Smith and Boyd Millen were on course for a quick anti-clockwise round. By the final peak, they realised they might beat Peter Walkington's 1971 record. Peter himself was pacing over the final leg and did not hesitate to urge the pair down to Keswick. They shaved five minutes off his time.

In 1976, John North completed most of his round with a repaired shoe and half of it without a watch. 'You're doing OK,' was all pacer Alan Heaton would say whenever John asked for his time. This was quite the understatement: he ended up breaking the record by 50 minutes, reducing it to 19 hours and 48 minutes.

Two months later, four members of the Bland family – Billy, Anthony (cousin), Chris (another cousin) and David (brother) – and Howard Pattinson set out from Keswick on a clockwise round under a perfect moonlit sky. The group stayed together over the initial legs, but by Bowfell the elastic had snapped and Billy was the leading Bland. In the end, while Chris was forced to retire (he made it round the next year), the remaining four joined the Club that day, albeit at different times. 'We arrived at Keswick… downed two bottles of cider, and I said: "never again",' wrote Billy in his report.

Billy completed in 18 hours and 50 minutes, taking 58 minutes out of John North's time, although there was a feeling he could have gone faster as a sole contender. His later decision to go again was undoubtedly influenced by Mike Nicholson when, in 1977, he made it round in 17 hours and 45 minutes, beating Billy's record by over an hour – a rare occurrence in any fell running history.

PUSHING BOUNDARIES

Once a standard is set, it does not take long for people to try to find new ways to test themselves against it. The Bob Graham was no different and the 1970s saw the creation of a series of associated challenges.

While the principle of support from others was core to the spirit of the Club, there was no prohibition on pursuing unofficial endeavours in an individual capacity. In 1973, Steve Poulton was the first to try for a solo round, supported only at the four road crossings. The longer you travel on your own, the harder it gets and Steve also had to contend with worsening weather over the penultimate leg. The margins grew tighter on every successive summit. He reached Robinson with success still a possibility, but the descent proved exasperatingly slow. In the darkness and mist, with only a failing torch for assistance, the remaining minutes ticked away and ultimately elapsed on the long run back to Keswick. Two years later, Steve made a second solo attempt and made it round successfully.

If there is a sea between having pacers and going solo, there is an ocean between having supporters and complete self-reliance. In 1977, Alan Walker succeeded in the first solo and unsupported round, and in far from good weather. The fact that he started and finished in Threlkeld did nothing to diminish from the achievement (qualifying rounds must start and finish at the Moot Hall).

In 1977, Boyd Millen succeeding in completing a round from the Moot Hall. Then he did another, after only an hour of rest in between. The first of his circuits was clockwise (in under 21 hours) and he then went the opposite direction (in just over 30 hours). Collectively, they comprised the maiden 'double round', a feat which has been repeated on only a handful of further occasions. Two years later, Roger Baumeister undertook the same challenge with a novel adjustment: he went clockwise from Keswick to Yewbarrow, but then turned back and travelled anti-clockwise through Keswick and back to Yewbarrow, before returning clockwise to Keswick. Roger set off on a Friday night, for the simple reason that he had to be back at work on Monday morning. Either

Left: Peter Walkington
Right: Joss Naylor beginning the ascent of Steel Fell on his 1975 Fell Record
Bottom: Roger Baumeister (standing right) at Wasdale on his double round (Martin Stone)

because of, or in spite of, the timetable, he completed the double in under 48 hours.

Meanwhile, Stan Bradshaw also stepped up to complete a brace of Bob Grahams. Seventeen years earlier, he had finished his first and he was now embarking on a second to celebrate his 65th birthday. He finished with only a handful of seconds to spare, becoming the then oldest person to have completed a round.

The recognition of age was also the genesis for a new type of round, that of matching one's age with one's peaks. Endurance challenges have never been the preserve of the young – Bob Graham had been 43 and Eustace Thomas 53 when they set their records – and so the quest for symmetry was a natural progression. In May 1977, Eddie Hill completed a circuit of 50 peaks to mark his 50th year. Over the following decades, the concept would be extended by a small number of accomplished veterans to mark the ages of 55, 60 and even 70. There is no formal record; it is simply a personal celebration and the choice of tops is a matter for each individual.

By 1977, the age range for successful completers had spread as far as 48 years. At the other end of the spectrum was 17-year-old Steven Tosh. For a year, he had nourished the ambition to be the youngest person to join the Bob Graham Club. When the day came, it went without a hitch and he completed in under 23 hours. 'It was the proudest moment of my life,' he wrote in his report, 'spent in the company of the finest people I know.'

INAUGURAL WOMEN

1977 was the year of 'firsts': first solo and unsupported, first double, first under-18 and first over-65. But the most notable of them all was the successful completion by Jean Dawes, who became the first woman to join the Bob Graham Club.

Today, it is well known that the physical differences between women and men are significantly diminished over endurance distances and, in many cases, largely irrelevant. Some long-distance records have been set by women

Top: Jean Dawes approaching the Moot Hall at the end of her 1977 round
Left: Anne-Marie Grindley (Tommy Orr)
Right: Ros Coats (Tommy Orr)

A CLUB IS FORMED · 39

outright and there is a strong desire to pursue equality in all aspects of fell running. But in the 1970s, the longest distance Olympic women's event was the 1,500m and relatively few established fell races accepted women entrants on the same terms as men. Thankfully, the Bob Graham Club has never distinguished between men and women, and neither do the fells.

Jean's first attempt came in 1976. She went well until Wasdale, but then began to feel the effects, experiencing a bad patch going up Great Gable. Nonetheless, she remained largely on schedule up until Honister. She left the quarry at 9pm with three hours to go, committing to finish no matter what the time. Unfortunately, by the final peak she was 'asleep on her feet' and she arrived back 50 minutes after the 24 hours had elapsed. Everyone with her knew that she was capable of more.

She set out again a year later in June. Leg one was in rain and mist, but the weather did not dent progress. After a ten-minute rest in Threlkeld, the traverse of the Dodds was also made in the clouds. Boyd Millen supported from this point and ended up going with her all the way to Keswick (excellent preparation for his double round the following month). Fred Rogerson met her atop Seat Sandal before a 26-minute stop at Dunmail. Some fatigue-based doubt was creeping in, but she kept going. In a potentially problematic reprise of 1976, she nearly fell asleep on a Kirk Fell boulder, thankfully awoken by a shout from Boyd – 'we've lost her, where the hell is she?' There were no more mishaps and she made it back to the Moot Hall with over half an hour left on the clock.

At that year's reunion dinner, Jean was visibly moved as she received a standing ovation when presented with her certificate of membership. 'Fred Rogerson has a lot to answer for, encouraging us in these mad but beautiful days on the fells,' she said. 'Believe it when I say he has given us all some moments in our lives which are unforgettable.'

GRINDLEY EXTENDS

As with many outstanding athletic achievements, once they have been accomplished, they are soon repeated, and Anne-Marie Grindley was welcomed as the second woman of the Club in June 1978. 'Ladies: may I recommend the Bob Graham Round to you – all those lovely men waiting on you hand and foot!' she announced.

Nonetheless, the fells do not climb themselves. Anne-Marie benefited from fantastic weather and was up on schedule throughout, at one point even missing a pacer as she cruised through a road crossing earlier than planned. By the time she returned to the Moot Hall, she had knocked nearly two and a half hours off Jean's time. The round was all the more special for having been completed with her husband, Will.

Feeling that she could go further, Anne-Marie then set about initiating the women's Fell Record. Given the rules of the record, her choices would quite literally set the path that future record breakers would need to take. She discussed her additions with Fred Rogerson in advance, agreeing that a peak could be included in the Fell Record if it was surrounded by at least two 50-foot contours. 'As the first female to do more than 42, I felt it was my choice of route,' she said.

On the same June weekend of Anne-Marie's attempt, a large group of runners also assembled at the Moot Hall, including Ros Coats, who was after a fast round, and Roger Baumeister, who wanted two. The main risk was to the support teams rather than the contenders: in the midst of a fuel crisis, nearly all of Cumbria's filling stations had run dry. In two parallel challenges, cars were nursed to the roadside stops while the runners traversed the fells.

Anne-Marie completed a round of 58 peaks, just as Ros Coats finished her Bob Graham in a time of 20 hours and 31 minutes (despite taking a poor line between Blencathra and Great Calva). Anne-Marie had started the weekend with the Bob Graham record, had lost it, but had come away with a Fell Record that was to last for well over a decade. For her part, Ros had set the fastest women's Bob Graham time by over half an hour, in the same year that she took the crown in the inaugural British Women's Fell Running Championship. Later that year, Wendy Dodds became the fourth female member of the Club.

Collectively, Jean, Anne-Marie, Ros and Wendy demonstrated that the round was for all fell runners. Together with the men, they put the Bob Graham on its firmest foundation yet. Fewer than ten years on from the Club's establishment, there was no more danger that Bob Graham's achievement would be forgotten.

FIFTY YEARS ON

1980 – 1988

'One should never underestimate a person's will to achieve, nor should any record, however remarkable, be deemed unbeatable.'

Martin Stone

The 1980s brought the 50th anniversary of Bob Graham's 1932 record, a cause for great celebration. Seemingly unbeatable records were beaten and, in their place, seemingly unbeatable records were set. All the while, Club membership continued to rise, just as interest in sister rounds in Wales and Scotland began to spread.

CELEBRATING THE JUBILEE

The 1980s saw a steady increase in the number of people taking up fell running, in part fuelled by the 'marathon boom' and proliferation of race events. This all contributed to continued growth in the Club's membership – there were four times as many new completions in the 1980s as in the 1970s. Every round is an experience shared with others, so it was only natural that members inspired and encouraged further contenders to come forward. This was entirely consistent with the Club's ethos: you help others, others help you.

In 1982, the Club enjoyed a memorable year, with members coming from all over Britain to mark the 50th anniversary of the 1932 round. Forty of them took part in a relay around the 42 peaks, set off by Phil Davidson, one of Bob's original pacing team. Alan Heaton carried the baton out of Keswick and up

Skiddaw before handing it on. It continued to pass from runner to runner, with Jean Dawes completing the final stint, to be greeted by a large crowd in Keswick. Later that day, a memorial cairn was unveiled by Eva Graham, Bob's niece, near Ashness Bridge, on a piece of land once owned by the Graham family.

THE BLAND WAY

Billy Bland liked to say that the Bob Graham Round was just a walk. But that did not mean that he did not want to complete it as quickly as possible. While his 1976 round was a record at the time, he did not feel it was a true reflection of his best.

A second round was planned for 1982. By this point, 'King Billy' was at the height of his abilities, bookending the attempt with decisive race wins at Ennerdale and Wasdale, respectively. While he may have casually mentioned to pacers that 16 hours was a good target, there was deliberately no schedule; the strategy was simply to test himself against the fells and see how fast he could go.

Billy departed the Moot Hall at 5am on midsummer weekend. The first two legs were completed in under five hours; leg three was put to bed in under four hours. Only the very best fell runners could pace him and even then he was near-impossible to follow: Tony Cresswell was due to support from Rossett Pike, but he arrived slightly too late for the rendezvous and, despite fresh legs, took until Ill Crag to make the catch.

Joss Naylor assumed pacing duties from Wasdale, his first task being to deliver a hard shake to Billy's legs, supposedly to flush out the lactic acid from the lower limbs. 'There was nowt wrong with my legs, but he wanted to do it anyway!' Billy insisted. But by Grey Knotts, something really was wrong and he struggled with a lack of energy on the descent to Honister quarry. After a 13-minute rest, the final leg was dispatched in under two hours. Aside from the

Previous: Fred Rogerson, Eva Graham and Phil Davidson at the unveiling of Bob Graham's memorial cairn in Borrowdale (Brian Covell)

Top: Pete Barron and Billy Bland start the ascent of Clough Head (Billy Bland)

Middle: Running with pacers on the final section to Keswick (Billy Bland)

Bottom: Soon after finishing at the Moot Hall (Billy Bland)

momentary weakness at Honister, he had appeared entirely fresh throughout. The total time was 13 hours and 53 minutes, having incredibly managed to cleave nearly four full hours from the previous record. Only two months later, Billy's brother, Stuart, set the then second-fastest time of 14 hours and 56 minutes.

Billy's record would go on to stand for 36 years, longer even than Bob Graham's 1932 record. While the achievement was justly celebrated at the time, it was only over the ensuing years that it was realised quite what a mark had been set.

As the appreciation grew, Billy wanted to show that the round really was just the long walk it had been originally called back in the 1930s. In 1989, now largely retired from racing, he set off with 17-year-old nephew Gavin, this time going anti-clockwise. The objective was to have one foot on the ground at all times, walking the whole way. Just as in 1982, they went faster than envisaged and some pacers were missed. Both Blands finished within 21 hours, although Billy could not help but move ahead on the final descent. He complained that the walk led to his one and only 'running' injury, caused by having to hold back on the downhills. Nevertheless, he was pleased to have made his point and avuncularly concluded that he hoped it might 'encourage those who think they'll never be able to do a Bob Graham Round to see it in a different light. Have a go!'

SHORT DAYS IN LAKELAND

'The snow was so deep that it had filled in the crevices between large rocks… About halfway down, I felt myself slipping on the icy snow. I dug my heels in and fell over on my face. The weight of my boots swung me round and I went sliding down feet first… I clawed at everything to keep myself from gathering speed and going over the other side of Gable… I tore my finger ends, but fortunately I was able to keep myself from getting away.'

So reported Bob Graham, after a lucky escape in March 1937. He, like many others, knew winter offered a whole new way to experience the fells, albeit not without risk. Some 45 years later, in 1982, Club President Joss Naylor used his speech at the reunion dinner to advise the assembled membership against winter rounds – the oppressive long night, snow and ice could leave an unprepared contender in a perilous state. These were well-intentioned and probably wise words, but the allure of 42 snow-capped tops was too great for some to ignore.

The first winter attempt had actually taken place three years earlier, by Pete Simpson in 1979. He set out on the winter solstice on a joint attempt with Martin Stone. Going anti-clockwise, Scafell proved the deciding juncture: Martin had to retire and Pete was forced to make a slow descent by Foxes Tarn as Broad Stand glistened in beautiful yet deadly verglas. The lost time could not be made back, but Pete persevered to the end with a 26-hour completion.

Five years later, Selwyn Wright (future Club Chairman) revived the winter round. To enhance the experience, he chose to be supported only at road crossings. He was fully cognisant of the difficulties of solo mountaineering in the conditions – indeed, overcoming them was the very purpose of the challenge. Similar to Pete, all went well until leg three, when a blizzard on Scafell forced a tactical retirement. In winter, the mark of a successful round is one which ends at the right time, on the terms of the contender.

In 1985, Selwyn made a second attempt – again, like Pete, it was completed in longer than 24 hours. But it was third time lucky for him in 1986, this time with John Brockbank as a co-contender and a team of pacers. Success came on a day of perfect conditions, authentically winter but not prohibitive to running – the pair finished in 23 hours and six minutes. That very same season, Steve Parr repeated the feat with even less daylight, just one day before the winter solstice. Despite falling an hour behind schedule by Bowfell, he made back the time, all the more impressive for the fact that he covered four of the five legs without any support on the fells. Steve's 1986 success followed two attempts the previous winter, the second one ending with only one fell to go.

Two weeks after that, Martin Stone dispensed with both pacers and roadside support, completing the round in 19 minutes under the 24 hours. Some of Joss's words may have rung true during sketchy moments ascending Fairfield, Bowfell and Scafell. For the latter, Lord's Rake was filled with snow and Martin only made it up by fashioning fingerholds out of holes left by a previous ascender's ice axe. Quite apart from the considerable physical achievement, it was an extraordinary feat of mental endurance. The challenge was an attack on all the senses, which can be conveyed in no better terms than Martin's own recollection:

For 24 hours, every step is premeditated, the torch kept low as you check for glazed rock and pools of water ice. Each foot placement is with care as you skate across streams which have frozen and spread over large areas of hillside. The 27,000 feet of jarring descent is unyielding, even frozen earth feels like rock to a tired body. The occasional slip on dodgy ground serves to concentrate the mind after a lapse into the long-distance runner's dream world. Cold air numbs your face and mouth, it also chills the stomach. Freezing water destroys the sense of taste and food loses its attraction. Your feet soon feel numb, no longer providing you with the spring and agility you need.

'Is it really worth it?' he asks. Emphatically, yes. Standing atop the final summit, 'you pause awhile to look around you at 41 snowy peaks lit by a rising moon. You'd be a strange person not to be moved by the beauty and grandeur.'

ASCENT OF SUPERMAN

While the Bob Graham Club was going from strength to strength, the Lake District 24-Hour Fell Record lay untouched. Between 1960 and 1975, the Fell Record was improved on no fewer than eight occasions. It was inevitable that the arms race would at some point stall. That point seemed to have arrived with Joss's 72 peaks in 1975.

But this did not stop debate. While no one doubted the scale of the achievement, some of the peaks he added to the round did not meet with universal acceptance. Fells such as Little Calva and Coomb Height were of paltry prominence – in terms of both notoriety and topography. The discussion was not limited to the men's record: similar points were made in relation to some of the tops included by Anne-Marie Grindley in her 1979 round of 58 peaks.

Up until then, the one and only Fell Record rule had been that set out by Wakefield in 1906: to cover the most 2,000-foot peaks and return within 24 hours (although even that had been quietly ignored on a few occasions with fells such as Steel Fell and Aikin Knott). After much discussion, the Bob Graham Club made two important clarifications to the criteria. First, new

Top: Mark McDermott setting off up Yewbarrow on his 1988 Fell Record (Mark McDermott)
Middle: Mark (second left) celebrating with his team on his final peak (Mark McDermott)
Bottom: Returning to Braithwaite at the end of the round (Mark McDermott)

records must incorporate all the peaks of the last record. Second, any new peak must have at least a 50-foot drop in all directions.

This confirmed, all were keen for the record to be decided by the fells rather than a committee. Many assumed Joss's record would prevail. For a good number of years, they were right: six men tried and six men failed.

The first was Bill Smith, the formative fell running chronicler and an excellent runner in his own right. He succeeded in two long rounds of 55 and 63 peaks, both huge achievements but still almost ten peaks short of Joss's mark. John North, Paul Murray, John Blair-Fish and Martin Hudson then all tried, each without success. In 1983, Billy Bland was the final assailant, but he retired halfway round. He later admitted his heart was not in the endeavour and that he did not feel it was right to take the record from Joss. Maybe the 72 peaks really was unbeatable.

Mark McDermott had other ideas. Keen to pick up the gauntlet, he prepared a schedule for a seemingly audacious 76-peak round. To pull it off would require both meticulous planning and flawless execution. The former was delivered through months of careful reconnaissance and specific training; the latter began at 5am on 18 June 1988.

Starting from Braithwaite, Threlkeld was reached within four hours and with 11 summits topped, including the two extra peaks of Bowscale Fell and Bannerdale Crags. On he went over the Dodds, Helvellyn and Fairfield to Dunmail Raise, then Langdale followed, all while the heat of the day intensified. On Crinkle Crags, Mark was asked by a passing walker if he was doing a Bob Graham Round. 'I wish I was!' he called back. It was more like one-and-a-half Bob Grahams at a 17-hour pace.

So far, every summit had been reached within two minutes of the scheduled time. After putting the Scafell massif to bed, Mark still felt good. 'It's in the bag,' he quietly reassured Martin Stone at Wasdale – how many contenders can imagine being so sure with 27 fells to go? On Kirk Fell, they enjoyed a glorious sunset, which gave way to a clear, moonlit night over the north-western fells. As they reached Grisedale Pike, dawn broke and red tinges of sunrise guided the triumphant final descent.

Before he had set out, Mark was little known in fell running circles. Few thought he could do it, even among his support team. This was no personal slight; it was simply an assumption that the record could only be broken by a hardened fell racer. That all changed when he returned to Braithwaite with a new Fell Record set: 76 peaks in 23 hours and 26 minutes. 'Ascent of superman,' headlined Chris Brasher's article in the national press. As one of Joss's Fell Record pacers, he was well-placed to judge.

BEYOND THE ROUND

For most, completing the Bob Graham is the culmination of a quest. For others, it simply demonstrates that more is possible. There have been no shortage of Club members whose qualifying rounds have been the start of something, rather than the end. The beauty of the fells and open country is that the possibilities are limitless; this freedom is one of the fundamental attractions of fell running.

The concept of matching age and peaks had been inaugurated in the 1970s with the '50 at 50'. Come the 1980s, this was repeated on a number of occasions, reflecting that age is no hindrance to endurance. George Brass pushed this to '55 at 55' in 1988, the first person to do so. George's most memorable accomplishment had been to be the only man to finish the 1962 Lake District Mountain Trial in appalling conditions, traipsing into Glenridding, clutching one disintegrated shoe and wearing the other. It was a race that even Eric Beard, Stan Bradshaw, Ken Heaton and 'Iron Joss' failed to complete.

In 1984, Steve Parr created a single, uninterrupted round of the Lake District's 61 2,500-foot peaks. The route gave a more complete tour of the high places in Lakeland than the Bob Graham, incorporating the Coniston, High Street and Grasmoor ranges. Steve took 43 hours to complete the circuit in very mixed weather conditions, an achievement that would not be bettered until 2020. He was also an accomplished climber, but tragically disappeared in the Himalaya mountains in 1990. Fittingly, the circuit of the 2,500-footers is now recognised as the Steve Parr Round, ensuring his name lives on.

The following year, even this 61-summit round was eclipsed. When Alfred Wainwright published his seven pictorial guides covering 214 fells, he would have thought it anathema to make a continuous traverse of all the summits. But while fell runners appreciate the landscape no less than walkers, they have different ways of enjoying it. Chris Bland was the first to attempt this ultimate expedition, neatly aiming to bag all the fells from Wainwright's seven books in seven consecutive days, with the added constraint of returning to his home in Borrowdale each night for a brief rest. By the end of the week, he had managed to visit 192 of the 214 tops. In 1985, Alan Heaton consolidated all the fells into a single, more logical route. Just under ten days and one mid-round hospital visit later (to receive a course of antibiotics for an inflamed foot), he had recorded the fastest completion of all the Wainwrights. The next year, Joss Naylor succeeded in touring all 214 fells in just over seven days (demonstrating the huge challenge of Chris's original plan). The majority of Joss's round was completed in heatwave conditions. While the weather broke on the sixth day, Joss did not, although he was forced to go into the darkest of places to finish.

Further afield, the Bob Graham was inspiring similar rounds in other mountain regions, most notably Snowdonia and the Highlands of Scotland. In Wales, the Paddy Buckley – or Welsh Classical Round – was born out of a desire to link up the most prominent of Snowdonia's peaks in a natural circuit. While it was Paddy who led its invention, Wendy Dodds was the first registered completer in 1982.

The Scottish round was an evolution of Tranter's round, an existing tour of the Munros around Glen Nevis, which was extended by five mountains to make it 24 peaks in 24 hours. It was devised by Charlie Ramsay after a chance encounter with Chris Brasher while on a family holiday to the Lake District in 1977. Charlie had offered to help carry supplies up Skiddaw in support of one of Chris's Bob Graham attempts. He was then asked to do the rest of leg one and, one leg after the other, simply kept going, making use of Chris's pacers despite his early retirement. In the end, Charlie completed the entire round 'on sight', with zero preparation. After a well-deserved congratulatory dinner, Chris challenged him to concoct a sister round for Scotland. Thus, the Ramsay was born. Just like the Bob Graham and the Lake District 24-Hour Fell Record, Ramsay's Round and the Scottish 24-Hour Munros Record now have separate but parallel histories.

The indefatigable Martin Stone was the first person to complete all three of the rounds in under 24 hours, which he did by June 1987. Now known as the 'big three', the Bob Graham seed had been sown in each nation of mainland Britain, with countless new opportunities for mountain endeavour. The Bob Graham Round seeks no monopoly and the more it inspires, the better.

A NOTABLE RETIREMENT

1989 – 1999

> 'Whenever I am faced with something impossible, the thought springs up irrepressibly: "But I have done the Bob Graham!" The impossible never seems quite so hard again.'
>
> **Selwyn Wright**

Fred Rogerson had been the Club's driving force since its establishment in 1971. He began it with only a handful of others; he passed it on with well over a thousand members. This was the decade of his retirement and the end of an era.

OUTRIGHT WOMEN

By the early 1990s, fewer than 50 women had joined the Bob Graham Club. But this did not stop some of the most noteworthy stories coming from within their ranks. One who did more than most was Hélène Diamantides (now Whitaker), who completed three Bob Grahams in three consecutive years.

Hélène came to fell running while at university, having been introduced to the sport by Alison Wright. In 1987, the pair set a record for running the 188-mile route from Everest Base Camp to Kathmandu. Two years earlier, Alison had joined the Bob Graham Club as its then youngest woman member (at the age of 19). For her part, Hélène completed a solid qualifying round on her return from Nepal.

Come 1988, Hélène decided to go for a solo and unsupported round, partly because no woman had yet done it and she felt the gap should be filled. She was also attracted to going at her own pace, which in the end proved quick: despite not intending to push, she ended up slicing 14 minutes from Ros Coats's record with a time of 20 hours and 17 minutes. '[It was the] best day out in the hills I ever had,' she said.

The next year, pushing was the first and only item on the agenda. This time with pacers, she set out at midnight for a clockwise round, returning to the Moot Hall after 19 hours and 11 minutes, over an hour quicker than her solo round. This was quite something in its own right, but it was merely the final part of a trilogy which had begun just 72 days earlier. Back in June, Hélène had carved a full two hours from the overall record for the Paddy Buckley Round. Then, in July, she set another overall record for Ramsay's Round (this time by an hour, although Adrian Belton knocked off a further hour only 18 days later). After Martin Stone, Hélène was the second person to complete each of the 'big three' in under 24 hours. Fittingly, the pair went on to jointly win the inaugural Dragon's Back race in 1992. Her old Everest partner, Alison, also went on to complete a very fast Bob Graham, second only to Hélène's.

Hélène's achievements were all the more notable for the fact that she set overall records by such large margins. She was at the vanguard of a new generation of women fell runners who were leading the charge over the long rounds. Anne Stentiford (now Johnson) was next, taking the overall Paddy Buckley record in 1991, Martin Stone having secretly prepared a record schedule which she was persuaded to adopt during the attempt itself.

After Hélène's sequence, it was no surprise to see Anne assemble at the Moot Hall only four weeks later. This time she set off with every intention of going for a record. But it was a cold, wet day and morale was flagging until some nourishment and encouragement from Fred Rogerson at Dunmail Raise spurred her to Wasdale. The weather then deteriorated further, with storm-force winds hitting between Pillar and Great Gable. The choice of line was dictated solely by which terrain offered the most shelter; Kirk Fell had to be summited on all fours.

Top: Hélène Diamantides and Martin Stone at the finish of the 1992 Dragon's Back (Rob Howard)
Bottom: Anne Stentiford celebrates on the final fell of her 1994 Fell Record (Anne Johnson)

Fred had driven up to Honister in full expectation of driving down with Anne in the passenger seat. As his parked car was rocked by gusts, he set in for what might be a long wait. But Anne was resolute and somehow even ahead of schedule. Torrential rain came down on the final leg, but it need not have bothered as it was now clear that Anne would set a record. She took 22 minutes from Hélène's time, becoming the first woman to go under 19 hours.

Come July 1994, Anne set out on a circuit 20 fells longer, attempting to add four peaks to Anne-Marie Grindley's Fell Record of 58 fells. As the round progressed, the day became hotter, making eating a struggle. By the time she had topped Great Gable, three peaks had been added to the round – Catstycam, Lingmell and Haycock. One more was needed to make the target, but, with time tight, Fleetwith was ignored on the way down to Honister. Come the penultimate leg, Anne managed to build a margin over the Buttermere fells and so realised she could fulfil her ambition of 62 peaks by adding Grasmoor on the hoof. This she duly did. As she finished the round, she became one of the very few people to hold simultaneously the Fell Record and Bob Graham titles. Both records would stand for more than 20 years.

MARK HARTELL'S EXTRA PEAK

Anne's journey to the Fell Record had begun at Macclesfield Harriers, alongside fellow fell runner Mark Hartell. The pair trained together for their respective attempts on the women's and men's records, plotting routes and testing lines. While Anne secured her 62 peaks, Mark's target of 77 proved more elusive.

His first attempt was in July 1993. Poor conditions meant he had to retire at Dunmail Raise, eight hours into the round, 20 minutes down on schedule and having missed a peak in dense mist. '[He was] beaten by the Lakeland weather rather than the size of the challenge,' said Martin Stone. Mark went again in 1994, but the attempt turned awry with a navigational error on Coomb Height.

The dream was not over but he needed some time away from the record to come back fresh. This he did in 1997: fitter, stronger and primed. He set off from Braithwaite in tricky conditions, losing time over the northern fells which

Top: Mark Hartell at a 'rolling stop' during his 1997 Fell Record (Mark Hartell)
Bottom: Mark sprinting to the Moot Hall at the end of his 1999 round (Mark Hartell)
Overleaf: Andrew Chamings descending Hall's Fell ridge

A NOTABLE RETIREMENT • 57

had caused his downfall three years earlier. But he made back the time and was only one minute down by Threlkeld. Here, a decision was made. He had been over each part of the route at record pace at least eight times in preparation. Now was the time to put faith in the plan and run to schedule rather than feel.

Catstycam was added as the 77th peak and the schedule was still intact at Dunmail. This boded well given past attempts, despite the fact that the weather remained poor. Mark McDermott had flown in from the Middle East and was waiting to wish him well. Hartell paused for only brief moments; both Marks were known for taking 'rolling stops' rather than actual breaks.

He was starting to feel the effort by the time he reached the Langdales, though this coincided with better weather, which made for better going. There was a brief moment of concern when, after benefiting from a push up Broad Stand, it was unclear whether he could haul his pacer up after him. But it all came good. At Wasdale, McDermott was ready to pace.

Onto the final leg and there was still time in hand, but not much. There was even less after Mark lost ten minutes on Grasmoor. The tight margin made for a tense approach to Grisedale Pike, the final peak – another error could have brought the whole attempt crashing down. The agitating endgame was in stark contrast with Mark McDermott in 1988, who had been able to take time to celebrate on the last top.

Mark sprinted the last 300 yards and nearly 20 people in Braithwaite were waiting to receive him at 4.47am, with 13 minutes left on the clock. The seed sown at Macclesfield all those years earlier had grown into a record that would stand for 23 years.

BILLY BLAND'S CHALLENGE

While Mark Hartell was showing that even supermen could be beaten, Club members were increasingly appreciating the brilliance of Billy Bland's 1982 record. The longer it stood, the more unassailable it seemed. It was all the more impressive for the fact it had been set with no yardstick.

In 1992, Mark McDermott had set out to test himself against Billy's record, but the attempt did not make it beyond Dunmail Raise. Come 1999, Mark Hartell was next to throw himself at the wall. The preparation was the antithesis of his planning for the Fell Record: he decided to go for it only a few weeks beforehand. He had been primed to compete in an American ultra marathon but was not able to start. Race-fit and ready, the Bob Graham was his alternative outlet.

Mark set off with a schedule based on Billy's times, but he was far from sure it was a feasible prospect. Two legs down, he was behind but not irretrievably. However, over the remaining legs the minutes continued to ebb away – there was no great mishap, just a gradual, accumulating deficit. On the final leg, he recalibrated his target: he could make the second-fastest time if he completed quicker than Stuart Bland's 14 hours and 56 minutes. Sprinting to the Moot Hall, the margin was two minutes in his favour.

Was Billy's time beatable? The chances seemed slim given that even the giants of the Fell Record could not get within an hour. A relay version of his record was established – the Billy Bland Challenge – and most teams struggled to match his time, even with a fresh pair of legs for each section.

While Billy's speed could not be matched, the period saw a rich range of other efforts. In 1992, the Club gained its youngest member: Ben Squibb from Cornwall, who was only 13 when he completed. Three years later, Alan Heaton set out at the age of 67 from the Moot Hall to celebrate the 35th anniversary of his first Bob Graham. Sadly, the day proved too hot and he was forced to retire. The next year, Joss Naylor celebrated his 60th year with a linear traverse of 60 tops in less than 36 hours, covering most of the 2,500-foot peaks. Earlier in the decade, he had established 'Joss's fun run', also known as the Joss Naylor Challenge, a point-to-point from Pooley Bridge to Greendale Bridge in Wasdale, specifically for veteran runners. As of today, it has registered around 300 completions.

In 1993, Andrew and Louise Chamings completed a round in a time of 79 hours and three minutes. Seventeen years earlier, Andrew had suffered a serious spinal injury that rendered him paraplegic. With the aid of elbow crutches and callipers, he covered the round over ten days, accompanied by Louise, including a descent of Hall's Fell ridge from Blencathra. In recognition of the effort, the couple were given associate membership of the Club, an honour bestowed only to a very small number of individuals who go above and beyond in support of the Bob Graham.

That same year, Alison Crabb became the first woman to complete a winter round, in the same year as her qualifying summer round. The prospects were initially bleak as a prior recce revealed ridges paved in sheets of ice. Thankfully, much had thawed by the time Alison reached the tops, although Scafell was a tricky transition and gale-force winds hit on Steeple. She finished in 23 hours and 51 minutes. Seven years later, Nicky Lavery set a new women's mid-winter record with a round in early January of 22 hours and 45 minutes. She experienced near-perfect weather and a full moon lit her way over the night sections.

A THOUSAND APPRECIATIONS

The nature of the Bob Graham challenge is that retirements are a common affair. The road crossings at Dunmail, Wasdale and Honister have all seen their share of graceful exits. But 1998 saw the most notable of departures, this time from the Shap Wells Hotel: Fred Rogerson was standing down as Chairman of the Club.

Fred was born in Kentmere and lived near Windermere for all his life. He was a man of many passions, but he chose to devote himself to what he termed 'mountain endeavour'. Like Harry Griffin, Fred was one of the few people to

Top: Fred offering advice to Joss Naylor

Bottom: Fred (right) with Ken and Alan Heaton, preparing for an attempt (Fred Rogerson)

A NOTABLE RETIREMENT · 61

latch onto the scale of Bob Graham's 1932 achievement and keep it alive in people's memories until a contender was able to beat the record in 1960.

Fred ran the Club for close to 28 years. At the beginning, he planned a bulk order of 100 membership certificates, thinking that it would see him through to the millennium. Harry wisely bid him up to 200. Both were serious underestimates: in actuality, the Club welcomed its one thousandth member in 1996.

The four-figure roll call reflected the development of fell running as a sport, the growing appeal of endurance challenges and the popularity of the Lake District. But, above all, it reflected the efforts of Fred. 'I felt that there were other people out there who could do what Bob Graham and Alan Heaton had done,' he said. 'I wanted to encourage them.' He advised hundreds of runners and spent countless hours supporting at road crossings. He saw contenders at the worst of times and at the best of times, his motivating words often being the difference between failure and triumph.

The 1998 reunion therefore truly marked the end of an era. 'To be actually in at the grass roots – to conceive an idea and see it materialise – I can't put it into words,' he recounted with satisfaction. To honour his retirement, the Club compiled a book of articles, letters and poems by members as a tribute, presented by Mark Hartell, the Club's President. To quote from one: 'If I'd never become aware of, and involved in, Fred's strange obsession, I'd know a lot less about myself, about the fells and about my fellow man than I do now.'

The ovation that followed was spontaneous and prolonged; many hardened fell runners were moved to tears. The occasion was also tinged with the great sadness that Fred's beloved wife, Margaret, who died three years earlier, was not present to share the moment with him. They were a wonderful couple, whose selflessness and dedication touched the lives of so many.

Fred would sadly pass away in 2010, a few weeks before his 90th birthday. The next year, a group of 70 proudly escorted his ashes on a relay round. Appropriately, they were carried in a pocket watch case that had been gifted by Bob Graham to Phil Davidson, his friend and pacer. The homecoming runners were joined at Portinscale by a dozen members of the Rogerson family on the final leg to the Moot Hall. It was a wonderful memorial to Fred, whose spirit had now traversed the round to which he had devoted so much of his life.

AGE OF ENDURANCE

2000 – 2019

*'We had set out to achieve something together,
a pointless thing that wouldn't change the world,
but would change our world somehow for the better.'*

Allan Greenwood

The retirement and passing of Fred Rogerson marked a generational change. No man had done more to help the round and its ethos live on. But the community he created was dedicated to continuing his work and the Club did not skip a beat. As the membership surpassed 2,000 people, it became increasingly important to maintain the ethos and traditions of the round.

MOUNTAIN MARATHONS

In 2001, Cumbria was devastated by foot and mouth disease, and the fells were closed for most of the season. For the first time in 30 years, there were no new completions and it took some time for normal service to resume.

The peak in new members had come in the 1980s, driven by the marathon boom and growth in fell races. Following this rapid rise, the number of completions declined over the 1990s and 2000s. This was no cause for concern; the round and Club were still there for those who wanted them.

In parallel, entries to the longer Cumbrian fell races were waning, with fell runners seemingly preferring the shorter courses. The Lakeland classics have a

special quality, with many traversing over sections of the round. Happily, they are now thriving again, in part through the establishment of a specific championship to promote these prestigious events.

Their recovery may also be explained by the second running boom: the rise of 'ultra'. Adventure has always appealed to the human spirit – the timelessness is clear from the 200-year history of the Fell Record. But it has never been so accessible or desired. Over the 2000s, the interest in endurance challenges grew considerably, especially in mountain regions. This brought a new interest in the Bob Graham and other Lake District endeavours. While far from traditional Cumbrian parlance, the round was the original Lakeland 'ultra marathon'. A further catalyst was the prominence of Richard Askwith's wonderfully evocative *Feet in the Clouds*, which included an account of his personal quest to complete the round, which he did on his fourth attempt.

For the first time, a large number of potential new members were coming to the round without a fell-racing background. This was no more or less valid a journey, but it was a marked change. The result was that the 2010s witnessed the highest level of new completions in any past decade.

RECORDS FALL AND STALL

The emergence of ultra running may also have been one reason for the resurgence of interest in the Fell Record. Since the early 1980s, only two men and one woman had pushed for the record. That was about to change.

The women were the first to break cover, led by Nicky Spinks, who came to the record six years after her qualifying Bob Graham and five after recovery from breast cancer. Just like McDermott and Hartell, Nicky immersed herself in the route and detailed planning. Building on Anne Johnson's (née Stentiford) 1994 round of 62 peaks, she selected Fleetwith Pike and Sand Hill as her primary additions, with Grisedale Pike as a desirable extra.

Going clockwise, dawn broke over the first leg, bringing what would be a hot day. Nicky gained time traversing the initial northern fells, perhaps because Anne had completed them in the dark. She then flew down the 'parachute

Left: Nicky Spinks on her 2015 record round (Lee Procter)
Right: Jasmin Paris approaching Scafell summit on her 2016 record round (Jon Gay)
Overleaf: Joss Naylor congratulating Nicky at the finish of her double round (Nick Cable)

route' off Blencathra, arriving in Threlkeld 25 minutes up on schedule. Leg two also went well, in spite of the temperature. Anne then met her on Harrison Stickle to spur her on. Further minutes were gained over the Scafells and Gables, with Fleetwith safely brought into the round. The north-western fells were a greater challenge and there was deemed insufficient time to add Grisedale Pike after a poor line off Robinson. But, in the end, Nicky completed her 64 peaks comfortably within the 24 hours.

The going was harder on the men's side. Just like Joss's record of 72 peaks, Mark Hartell's 77 peaks were proving incredibly difficult to improve upon. Steve Birkinshaw made two attempts in 2009 and 2010, both of which ended in retirement. It is a measure of both Steve's quality and the strength of Mark's record that Steve would go on to beat Joss Naylor's landmark Wainwrights record in 2014.

The next assailant was Adam Perry, who alongside Alan Heaton should surely hold the title for most dedication to the Fell Record. The cruel difference is that Alan took the record on three separate occasions, while Adam did not quite manage to secure it on any of his four attempts.

In 2014, Adam gained 77 peaks but was not able to finish within the 24 hours; he had reached the summit of Grisedale Pike in 23 hours and 59 minutes. Nevertheless, it was a phenomenal achievement for a first attempt. In 2015, he was forced to retire on Yewbarrow in the heat. In 2016, an agonising navigational error off Green Gable put paid to success. The 2017 attempt was the final and perhaps closest of them all. Starting at 4am, it was good running despite frequent bad weather, right until the end, when Adam lost ten minutes on Hopegill Head and Whiteside due to poor visibility and slippery rocks. At 3.47am, he reached the final peak of Grisedale Pike, but timed out one mile from the finish at Braithwaite on the descent. He finished in 24 hours and 15 minutes. Had the envelope not been pushed quite so far, Adam's achievements would have been more than enough for the record in nearly every previous decade.

COMING BACK STRONGER

Not even Alan Heaton made four attempts in four consecutive years. But Adam's successive efforts are testament to both his spirit and the traditions of the Club. It should come as no surprise that he was paced by Mark Hartell and he himself would go on to pace the next record holder in 2020.

Of course, most Club members do not set records. The story of the round is far more about the grit, sweat and pain that goes into returning to the Moot Hall within 24 hours; the number of rounds finished in 23 hours 57 minutes, 58 minutes and even 59 minutes shows the scale of the test. But the membership roll contains no times: a completion is a completion. All members are equal.

Just as many fail as succeed – and yet the vast majority return. Once the round bites, it is very difficult to move on until the challenge is fulfilled. 'Failure' is simply success postponed, all the sweeter for the satisfaction of coming back stronger.

While just one example from countless contenders, the story of Allan Greenwood conveys the spirit perfectly. In 2005, following weekend after weekend of preparation and training, his round did not even make it to Wasdale. A plan for a second attempt was immediately put in motion, but it was not instigated by Allan; instead, Anne Johnson, the then women's Fell Record holder, took charge and put all the arrangements in order. The first

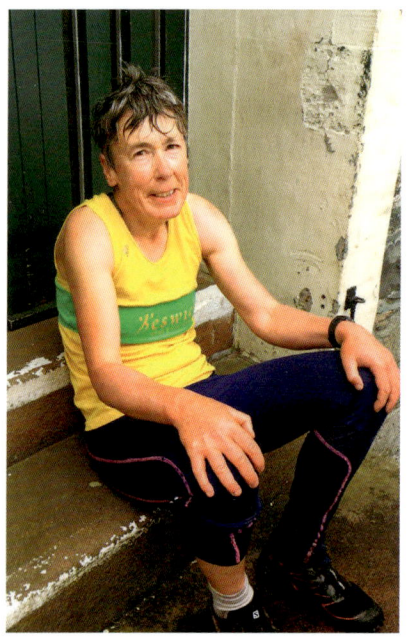

three legs of this round went well. On leg four, Allan was paced by two runners he had never met before – they would go on to become firm friends. After battling terrible weather, those same pacers encouraged him straight through Honister without a stop. He summited Robinson with one hour to go, pushed as hard as he could, but he tapped the Moot Hall door 23 minutes too late. Down but far from out, later that year, Allan completed the round on his third attempt, supported by many who had paced his earlier efforts.

Repeat attempts are not the preserve of 'everyday' Bob Graham contenders; they are just as much a feature for elite runners on their greater challenges. Everyone is pushing themselves to their own personal limit, indeed part of the attraction is the uncertainty of whether a goal can be achieved.

The thin line between success and failure is particularly present in challenges such as winter rounds. In the deep February snow of 2013, Jim Mann was forced to abandon his attempt on the winter record while traversing the Helvellyn ridge. But he was delighted: he knew that in better conditions he could break the record. Jim's story is one of a longstanding trial with the winter round, beginning in 2010. After a series of attempts and interim successes, he took the winter record in December 2013 with a time of 18 hours and 18 minutes. He hardly stopped at the road crossings and his strength was such that he was in better shape at Wasdale than Dunmail.

Kim Collison could not match Jim's record when he set out in December 2017, admittedly in quite different and deep snow conditions. But he returned in December 2019 with an astounding time of 15 hours and 47 minutes – the 12th fastest overall, in any season.

By now, the Club distinguished between 'winter' rounds (any completion in December, January or February) and 'mid-winter' rounds (a window of a few weeks around the winter solstice). The purpose of this separation is to reflect that the amount of daylight and degree of winter conditions greatly dictate the nature of the challenge. Of course, the calendar is merely a proxy for severity and it is better to celebrate each round on its own terms. The current mid-winter record is held by Andy Berry, who made it round in 18 hours and 41 minutes in early January 2017.

Top: Adam Perry approaching Harrison Stickle on his 2014 Fell Record attempt (Lee Procter)
Left: Julie Carter at the Moot Hall after her '55 at 55' (Julie Carter)
Right: Kim Collison at the finish of his winter round (Becx Carter)

Age-related rounds also showed no signs of ceasing, despite the ever-advancing numbers. In 2002, Wendy Dodds completed the first recorded women's '50 at 50' ('53 at 51', to be precise). She sprinted up to the Moot Hall in 22 hours and 38 minutes, nearly an hour faster than her original round, way back in 1979. This brought great satisfaction: 'it really was much easier,' she claimed. In 2019, Julie Carter of Keswick Athletic Club took it a handful further to become the first woman to complete '55 at 55'.

For the men, Yiannis Triadimis completed the first '60 at 60' within 24 hours in 2005 – on his third attempt that year. He had joined the Club ten years earlier with a '50 at 50'. That same year, Joss Naylor ran his final Bob Graham leg as a pacer, over 40 years after his first, which was in support of Eric Beard's Fell Record in 1963. In 2006, he made a linear traverse of 70 tops to mark his 70th birthday. Come 2018, Ken Taylor became the oldest person to complete the Bob Graham. A fell racer for 50 years, the 72-year-old showed age is no impediment, despite recovering from serious illness ten years prior.

WOMEN'S SINGLES AND DOUBLES

By 2012, it had been over twenty years since either the men's or women's Bob Graham records had been broken. Not since Alan Heaton in 1960 had there been such a long period without someone going faster.

The drought was ended by Nicky Spinks, who used her 2011 Fell Record as the launch pad for a fast Bob Graham. She set off in July 2012 in mixed conditions. The first half was on schedule but the rain made for slippery rocks over the Scafell massif and a sketchy ascent of Broad Stand. In a bid to not lose time, an unsustainable pace broke the flow of leg four and it took until the Gables to get back into a rhythm. She ran straight through Honister, pausing later only to put on a Dark Peak club vest for the final run-in. The clock stopped at 18 hours and 12 minutes, some 37 minutes faster than Anne Johnson in 1991.

Like many others, Nicky came back for more. In 2015, an April start meant there was still snow nestling on the crags. Unfortunately, the majority of the round was frustrated when she cut her hand while descending Blencathra; the remaining 39 peaks were tough to navigate with only one good arm in play. But she still managed to improve on her 2012 record by six minutes.

Nicky had now followed in the footsteps of Hélène Whitaker (née Diamantides) and held the women's record for each of the 'big three'. What was left to achieve? 'I wanted something different, something longer and slow,' Nicky explained. The double Bob Graham was the answer, inspired by fellow Dark Peak runner, Roger Baumeister in 1979. No one had done a double since. To celebrate a decade free from cancer, a start was planned for 2016.

When she set out, conditions were perfect, but the mental challenge of the double is that every summit gained is a summit to be repeated some hours later. Joss Naylor came to see her at Yewbarrow, the point at which she turned back for Keswick, replicating Roger's inventive route. Now, every summit gained was one not to be revisited – at least until Keswick.

The briefest of naps at Portinscale provided disproportionate rejuvenation for the anti-clockwise trip to Yewbarrow and back. She touched in at the Moot Hall 45 hours and 30 minutes after she originally embarked – the fastest ever double round. Nicky went on to complete a double Paddy Buckley and a double Ramsay's Round, the only person to have even attempted this, let alone succeeded.

Jasmin Paris paced Nicky over many of these record runs. While her specialism was racing – the longer and rockier, the better – an apprenticeship was in train. She was ready to aim for a Bob Graham record in spring 2016.

Jasmin set off from the Moot Hall at 4am under a full moon. By the time dawn broke over the heather of Great Calva, it was clear she was running far faster than the 17-hour schedule. Thankfully, the pacing team was able to bring forward their plans. Once the Scafells were reached, her knowledge of the Wasdale fell race route boosted both morale and speed – from then, neither faltered. Back at Keswick, Jasmin clocked in at an incredible 15 hours and 24 minutes, taking a huge chunk out of the women's record, reminiscent of Billy Bland's 'run to feel' in 1982. Amazingly, she was not a spent force at the end and wondered whether she could have extracted more. But, this time with echoes of Ken Heaton in 1961, she concluded nobly: 'I don't think one can relive a day like that. Some things are better left as they are, and I have a feeling this is one of them.'

A CATALAN IN CUMBRIA

While the women's record had been lowered three times in four years, Billy's record remained standing. While the passing of years had heightened its pedestal, Jasmin's lightning-quick round was an important reminder that no record was unbreakable.

Rob Jebb gave another cause for optimism later that year. Like Jasmin, he had generally favoured fell races instead of long rounds (and he also held the record for the Fred Whitton Challenge, road cycling's closest analogy to the Bob Graham). But he was inspired to try for a fast round after he paced one of Adam Perry's Fell Record attempts. Rob used a combination of Jasmin's, Billy's and Mark Hartell's schedules to guide him to a new second-fastest time of 14 hours and 30 minutes. At last, Billy's record was just about in sight. Honourable mentions must also go to Mark Palmer, who completed a sub 15-hour round in 2011, and Ryan Smith, who logged a new second-fastest time of 14 hours and 17 minutes in 2017 (running solo for part of the round and therefore not qualifying for Club membership).

Rob planned a second attempt in 2018, with one eye on improving his time and the other on beating Billy's record. A date was set for July and a formidable team of pacers was arranged. In the end it was not to be. The cause was weather: deciding that it was too hot for a Yorkshireman, Rob gracefully withdrew. In a truly magnanimous gesture, he then lent his support and team to another runner who was struggling to find pacers.

That contender was Kilian Jornet, a newcomer to Lakeland but not to the mountains. From his earliest childhood, he had lived and breathed alpine endeavour, in the process becoming one of the most celebrated international mountain runners of his time. A student of the sport's history, the 30-year-old Catalan had wanted to do the round for nearly a decade. However, circumstances only fell into place on 7 July 2018; sheer chance meant this was the same weekend as Rob's planned attempt.

Pacers secured, Kilian sought to pay his respects to Billy Bland, keen to emphasise his desire to maintain the traditions and ethos of the round

Top: Kilian Jornet guided down Blencathra by Carl Bell on his 2018 record round (Mick Kenyon)
Middle: Greeted by Billy Bland at Dunmail Raise (Billy Bland)
Bottom: Celebrating with Billy at the end of the round (Tim Harper)

throughout his attempt. Billy was welcoming, even taking Kilian to view Bob Graham's newly renewed gravestone at Stonethwaite. Other than that, it was intended to be a low-key affair, organised by Martin Stone, pacer to Billy on his 1982 record.

Setting off at 6am, the legs went like clockwork. The season had been exceptionally dry, which made for firm terrain and fast running. The only incident of note was eerily similar to an event during Billy's round: seemingly pushing too hard at the end of leg four, Kilian was struck by fatigue and dizziness on the descent of Grey Knotts. He avoided a similar fate only by ordering himself: 'I cannot sit down here!' He quickly came round after a Honister fuelling, although his steer to the leg five pacers was 'maybe not so fast this time.'

Still, just as Billy had used the target of a sub-14-hour time to propel him through the final leg, so did Kilian. But this time it was sub-13. He dug deep, very deep. All the while, word of mouth led hundreds to gather in the Market Square to see him in. As he ran towards the Moot Hall, the sea parted and he touched the green door with a time of 12 hours and 52 minutes.

Billy was the first to greet him and the two record breakers shared a private moment despite the crowd. After all the years of anticipation, it was a fittingly authentic and respectful affair. The spirit epitomised something Fred once said: 'I don't care what sport you do or where you go; you'll never find camaraderie like you get on the fells.'

PROTECTING GRAHAM'S LEGACY

Records are there to be broken, by whomever from wherever. The experience of an overseas professional completing the fastest round showed that what matters is the spirit in which it is done. The Club does not seek either to persuade or dissuade completions. Instead, its role is to preserve the traditions, spirit and ethics of the round. As membership and popularity grow, this becomes increasingly important.

Each generation has its issues to contend. For the early pioneers, it was access to the fells and how to prove their exploits to a disbelieving community. For the post-war fell runners, it was toppling the divide between amateurs and professionals, and between men and women. At the time, those were all difficult matters, but they have now hopefully been consigned to the past.

Today, the technological, societal and sporting context is clearly very different from Bob Graham's or even Fred Rogerson's time. Social media, GPS, the rise of ultra running and the development of Lakeland tourism pose new challenges. To reflect on these issues is not an attempt to turn back the clock; it is a question of how to best protect and nurture the round so it can be enjoyed by future members in a similar way to how it has been appreciated in the past. Looking forward, the impact of the increasing popularity of the round and the effect on the natural environment is likely to become a prominent debate.

Fortunately, there is generally a consensus among the Bob Graham community. Long may it continue. So, while the Club's guidance notes make clear a number of points (including that rounds will not be ratified if they are guided for payment), remarkably few explicit interventions have been required to stay on the straight and narrow. The spirit of learning the round from others who have gone before, supporting new attempts and fostering respect for the fells has naturally won through. Each of us has a role to play. We can do far worse than ask, 'what would Fred do?'

2020 AND BEYOND

'The strength and nourishment I was given on that run feed me even now. It was not my own achievement, but the gifts of others that made me feel differently. My effort was repaid a thousand-fold.'

Julie Carter

2020 was atypical in so many ways. But not even a global pandemic could dim interest in the Bob Graham and the Fell Record. In one short summer, the round filled a gap that racing could not. It is too early to bring a proper perspective to the achievements of the year, but their quality will surely stand the test of time. The legacies of Bob, Fred and countless others still live on, indeed they are stronger than ever.

STAYING LOCAL

When Kim Collison helped pace Adam Perry on his desperately close attacks on Mark Hartell's Fell Record, a kernel of an idea formed: might Kim one day make a go of it? The thought was parked; other plans were made. But shortly after the first national coronavirus lockdown in spring 2020, he was in the form of his life. Adhering to travel restrictions meant staying on the Cumbrian fells: it was the perfect opportunity to push for 78 peaks.

This is what led Kim to set out from Braithwaite at 3am in July. The decision had been made only a few short weeks earlier, far from the multi-year preparations deployed by McDermott, Hartell and Perry. But there was enough

Previous top: Kim Collison at the end of his 2020 Fell Record (Steve Ashworth)
Previous bottom: Carol Morgan at the end of her 2020 Fell Record (Simon Franklin)
Above: Beth Pascall descending Blencathra on her record round (Sam Benard)

time to form a strategy: 'plan A' was to add Haycock to the record, 'plan B' was to add Fleetwith Pike and 'plan C' – the reserve – was simply to go quicker than Hartell over 77 rather than 78 fells.

Once he was away, Kim stopped only momentarily on two occasions, merely long enough to remove stones from his shoes. The weather was fine and the first legs went exceptionally well. He was 11 minutes ahead of schedule at Threlkeld, 14 by Dunmail and 30 by Wasdale. But the margins on the Fell Record are such that usually the schedule is there to be met, not outdone – was it sustainable?

Come Yewbarrow, the old adage rang true: there is no easy way out of Wasdale. 'My stomach started to give way. I felt like I was hitting the wall and this is when it became much harder,' recounted Kim. Plan A was out the window; it was too soon to risk taking time out of the bank. But by the end of the leg, the detour to Fleetwith Pike felt viable, so plan B was put into action.

The additional peak now secured within the schedule, he just had to keep to Mark's splits to make it back within the 24 hours. Initially manageable, progress became harder when darkness set in over the Newlands fells, with the 13 peaks of the Grasmoor massif left to top. Then the mist descended. Each transition involved a stressful search for the line and cairn. The past experiences of Adam Perry weighed heavily.

But while the stakes were high and the navigation tricky, it all came good. Kim reached the summit of Grisedale Pike with 40 minutes left to make the final descent. It was only then that he knew he was going to do it. He was back in Braithwaite after 23 hours and 45 minutes.

Not to be outdone, a few months later Carol Morgan stepped up to take on the women's record. An Irish ultra runner coached by Kim, she had completed a solo and unsupported round only one month earlier, making a point of doing it without either a GPS or watch.

For her Fell Record attempt, Carol began at midnight, safely dispatching leg one in the dark and making good going over the Dodds as dawn broke. The first struggle did not come until Bowfell, but it was quickly resolved with nourishment. As ever, Yewbarrow was tough, but it is especially hard on the women's round as a scrambling descent must be made off Stirrup Crag (as opposed to the trod to Dore Head). As with Kim, tensions rose on the final leg as it became darker and harder to find the lines. There was just – just – time to claim Grisedale Pike, the additional 65th peak, but the pressure was on for the descent. Dropping down to the quarry road, she forced herself to 'run, run, run'. And she did: clocking in with a mere two minutes and 47 seconds to spare. It was the tightest ever margin on any Fell Record, but no less a record for it.

SWIFT BRITS

Until 2020, there had never been two Fell Records set in a single year. In a season that became remembered for the 'fastest known time', many other Lakeland records fell. The Steve Parr Round secured four completions, with a new record from Howard Dracup (since bettered by Andy Berry in 2021). The Wainwrights Round saw its first female attempt by Sabrina Verjee (who had set the women's mid-winter Bob Graham record in 2018), which she finished in just under seven days. But shortly after the finish, she asked the community not to treat it as an official completion, because of assistance offered on a number of painful descents towards the end of the round. Still, it was quite the performance: just like Steve Birkinshaw in 2014 and Paul Tierney in 2019, she left everything out on the fells, pushing well beyond what most would consider the limit. Later in 2020, Mel Steventon became the first woman to complete the Wainwrights Round, with a record of 13 days and 12 hours. (In 2021, Sabrina went on to set the outright record when she summited all 214 fells in five days and 23 hours, breaking the six-day marker on her fourth attempt.)

There was more to come. Step forward Beth Pascall, a seasoned trail and ultra runner, less familiar on the fells but no less suited to them. By her own admission, she preferred racing, but there were no races. Instead, the unspent energies were put into the Bob Graham Round.

The schedule was based around Jasmin's record, less one critical minute. But a sub-hour ascent of Skiddaw quickly indicated that Beth's round would be no marginal improvement. Aside from a brief dip early in leg three, the splits kept going her way. A swift descent to Wasdale and an under-schedule ascent of Yewbarrow confirmed the record was on. Unlike the men, there was no Grey Knotts wobble and she was still able to push on the road section to Keswick. The clock stopped at 14 hours and 34 minutes, 50 minutes faster than Jasmin and the overall sixth fastest Bob Graham ever.

October is not an ideal month for a scamp across the fells, but it was what Ambleside-based George Foster had to play with. It proved near perfect: a glorious sunrise on the approach to Blencathra preceded a Brocken spectre over the Dodds and bone-dry rocks over the Scafell range. He was on a 14-hour schedule and hitting all the targets. Billy Bland liked to say that his record was given too much respect, that more should have been done by the local fell runners to try to claim it. Kilian had shown that Billy's time could be beaten, but could George also be faster? The hope of doing so spurred the final leg and took him to a time of 13 hours and 44 minutes, nine minutes faster than Billy. It was the perfect end to an all too brief season.

SWEET NECTAR

One of the Club's original traditions is that each member is asked to complete a short report of their round, which goes on to be recorded in the archives. Many of the most impressive runners take far longer to pen their words than to complete a round; many of those who only just make it round compose the most inspiring tales. Before he retired as Chairman of the Club, Fred Rogerson would compile all the reports and read them with his wife over the winter months – 'without a word of a lie they were nectar.'

This book has tried to tell the story of these stories, a story that will continue. Bob Graham would doubtless be delighted that so many have literally followed in his footsteps, pushed forward by his original inspiration and the enthusiasm of those who have helped them. Together, they all ensure that the Bob Graham Round continues to be a very special challenge and the Bob Graham Club a very special club.

FURTHER READING

There are many other written records of the Bob Graham Round and Lake District fell running challenges. Many of these publications have been important sources of information and inspiration for this text.

A number of Harry Griffin's books reflect on the early history of the Lake District 24-Hour Fell Record, in particular *In Mountain Lakeland* (1963). Between 1972 and 1978, Fred Rogerson produced a detailed account of all records and rounds in *History and Records of Notable Fell Walks in the Lake District*. The Club's original publication of *42 Peaks* (1982) tells the story up to the 50th anniversary of Bob Graham's round. Bill Smith's totemic *Stud Marks on the Summits* (1985) explains the parallel histories of the Bob Graham Round and the Fell Record. Peter Travis's *The Round* (1985) is a fictional story based on the round.

More recently, Richard Askwith's evocative *Feet in the Clouds* (2004) puts the Bob Graham in the context of the sport of fell running and is often credited with contributing to increased interest in the round. Steve Chilton's *The Round: In Bob Graham's Footsteps* (2015) tells the story of the round through a series of in-depth conversations with key players. Peter McDonald's *Tribute to the Round* (2020) focuses on the story behind the route of the round. Last but not least, *Fellrunner* magazine has published countless articles on all aspects of the round, from the 1970s to the present day.

Opposite: Head torches guide a night descent of Seat Sandal (Adam Lloyd)
Overleaf: Contenders ascend Great Gable from Beck Head (Jon Gorrigan)

RECORD TABLES

MEN'S FELL RECORD

Arthur Wakefield	1905	21 peaks
Cecil Dawson	1916	23 peaks
Eustace Thomas	1922	29 peaks
Bob Graham	1932	42 peaks
Alan Heaton	1960	42 peaks
Ken Heaton	1961	51 peaks
Alan Heaton	1962	54 peaks
Eric Beard	1963	56 peaks
Alan Heaton	1965	60 peaks
Joss Naylor	1971	61 peaks
Joss Naylor	1972	63 peaks
Joss Naylor	1975	72 peaks
Mark McDermott	1988	76 peaks
Mark Hartell	1997	77 peaks
Kim Collison	2020	78 peaks

WOMEN'S FELL RECORD

Jean Dawes	1977	42 peaks
Anne-Marie Grindley	1978	42 peaks

Anne-Marie Grindley	1979	58 peaks
Anne Stentiford	1994	62 peaks
Nicky Spinks	2011	64 peaks
Carol Morgan	2020	65 peaks

MEN'S BOB GRAHAM RECORD

Bob Graham	1932	23h 39m
Alan Heaton	1960	22h 18m
Peter Walkington	1971	20h 43m
Boyd Millen & Bill Smith	1973	20h 38m
John North	1976	19h 48m
Billy Bland	1976	18h 50m
Mike Nicholson	1977	17h 45m
Billy Bland	1982	13h 53m
Kilian Jornet	2018	12h 52m

WOMEN'S BOB GRAHAM RECORD

Jean Dawes	1977	23h 27m
Anne-Marie Grindley	1978	21h 05m
Ros Coats	1979	20h 31m
Hélène Diamantides	1988	20h 17m
Hélène Diamantides	1989	19h 11m
Anne Stentiford	1991	18h 49m
Nicky Spinks	2012	18h 12m
Nicky Spinks	2015	18h 06m
Jasmin Paris	2016	15h 24m
Beth Pascall	2020	14h 34m